Global Forum on Transparency and Exchange of Information for Tax Purposes Peer Reviews: United States 2011

COMBINED: PHASE 1 + PHASE 2

June 2011
(reflecting the legal and regulatory framework
as at February 2011)

OECD

This work is published on the responsibility of the Secretary-General of the OECD. The opinions expressed and arguments employed herein do not necessarily reflect the official views of the OECD or of the governments of its member countries or those of the Global Forum on Transparency and Exchange of Information for Tax Purposes.

Please cite this publication as:
OECD (2011), *Global Forum on Transparency and Exchange of Information for Tax Purposes Peer Reviews: United States 2011: Combined: Phase 1 + Phase 2*, Global Forum on Transparency and Exchange of Information for Tax Purposes: Peer Reviews, OECD Publishing.
http://dx.doi.org/10.1787/9789264115064-en

ISBN 978-92-64-11505-7 (print)
ISBN 978-92-64-11506-4 (PDF)

Series: Global Forum on Transparency and Exchange of Information for Tax Purposes: Peer Reviews
ISSN 2219-4681 (print)
ISSN 2219-469X (online)

Table of Contents

About the Global Forum

The Global Forum on Transparency and Exchange of Information for Tax Purposes is the multilateral framework within which work in the area of tax transparency and exchange of information is carried out by over 100 jurisdictions, which participate in the Global Forum on an equal footing.

The Global Forum is charged with in-depth monitoring and peer review of the implementation of the international standards of transparency and exchange of information for tax purposes. These standards are primarily reflected in the 2002 OECD *Model Agreement on Exchange of Information on Tax Matters* and its commentary, and in Article 26 of the OECD *Model Tax Convention on Income and on Capital* and its commentary as updated in 2004. The standards have also been incorporated into the UN *Model Tax Convention.*

The standards provide for international exchange on request of foreseeably relevant information for the administration or enforcement of the domestic tax laws of a requesting party. Fishing expeditions are not authorised but all foreseeably relevant information must be provided, including bank information and information held by fiduciaries, regardless of the existence of a domestic tax interest.

All members of the Global Forum, as well as jurisdictions identified by the Global Forum as relevant to its work, are being reviewed. This process is undertaken in two phases. Phase 1 reviews assess the quality of a jurisdiction's legal and regulatory framework for the exchange of information, while Phase 2 reviews look at the practical implementation of that framework. Some Global Forum members are undergoing combined – Phase 1 and Phase 2 – reviews. The ultimate goal is to help jurisdictions to effectively implement the international standards of transparency and exchange of information for tax purposes.

All review reports are published once adopted by the Global Forum.

For more information on the work of the Global Forum on Transparency and Exchange of Information for Tax Purposes, and for copies of the published review reports, please refer to *www.oecd.org/tax/transparency.*

Executive summary

1.   This report summarises the legal and regulatory framework for transparency and exchange of information in the United States as well as practical implementation of that framework. The international standard which is set out in the Global Forum's Terms of Reference to Monitor and Review Progress Towards Transparency and Exchange of Information, is concerned with the availability of relevant information within a jurisdiction, the competent authority's ability to gain timely access to that information, and in turn, whether that information can be effectively exchanged with its exchange of information partners.

2.   The United States is the world's largest economy and has a sophisticated regulatory environment. Its tax system, in particular, is highly complex and creates extensive obligations on all persons having economic connections with the United States to pay tax, report transactions, file returns (both tax returns and information returns), and generally subject themselves to the authority of the Internal Revenue Service (the IRS). The power of the IRS to compel information held by persons within its jurisdiction is very strong and its use for the purposes of exchange of information in tax matters is well supported by U.S. courts.

3.   The United States signed its first tax treaty in the 1930s, and now has an extensive network of exchange of information agreements that meet the international standards and that cover all relevant partners. Requirements for confidentiality and the maintenance of rights and safeguards are in place. The United States is also a founding signatory to the *Joint Council of Europe/ OECD Convention on Mutual Administrative Assistance in Tax Matters.*

4.   The United States processes a very large number of information requests each year in addition to a program of both spontaneous and automatic exchange. On average, the United States replies to approximately 1000 cases (each generally constituting multiple requests for information) per year, and automatically exchanges approximately 2.5 million items of information per year. The exchange of information unit within the IRS is generally well-trained and well-organised. Tax attachés in offices around the world facilitate exchange of information in certain key geographic areas. Guidelines for the

exchange of information provide for specific timelines in which EOI requests should be processed, including the provision of interim responses in complex cases.

5.   The United States' information exchange partners have indicated a general satisfaction with the U.S. exchange of information program. Specific issues have been raised regarding the availability of information in certain cases, and with the time required to process requests, in particular with regard to requests for banking information.

6.   The power of the IRS to obtain information for tax purposes is wide-ranging and is coupled with strong compulsory powers. Such powers are used regularly and the U.S. courts have been unequivocal in their view that these powers can be used to obtain information for the purpose of responding to a request for information under an information exchange mechanism.

7.   Regarding the availability of information, the legal and regulatory framework is generally in place for all entities and arrangements to maintain ownership and identity information through the application of its federal tax law provisions as well as applicable state law. Limited Liability Companies that have only one owner may be disregarded as entities separate from their owners for U.S. federal income tax purposes. Where the LLC has no U.S. owner, is not engaged in a U.S. trade or business, has no employees or activity in the United States (such as a bank or other financial account in the U.S), no U.S. source income, and is not otherwise subject to federal income taxes, employment taxes, or excises taxes, information on the owner of such an entity will not be available pursuant to U.S. federal tax laws. Information may be held in accordance with the statutory law of the state of the entity's formation, though this is not guaranteed in all cases. Changes have been introduced to certain federal information reporting rules affecting such entities, though it is not clear that these changes will guarantee that ownership information is available in all cases.

8.   Information concerning trustees, settlors and beneficiaries of trusts that are subject to federal income tax law, anti-money laundering law or state law is available. Tax law generally requires that adequate accounting records be maintained. However, requirements to maintain adequate accounting records do not necessarily apply to LLCs with only one owner that are not subject to the tax law or other record maintenance requirements.

9.   The U.S. tax system imposes a wide range of substantive tax and information reporting obligations. Persons seeking to obscure their affairs for tax or other reasons wouldn't generally be eager to expose themselves to the authority of the Internal Revenue Service.The legal and regulatory framework for exchange of information in the United States is in place. Certain circumstances do arise, in particular the case of certain LLCs with only one

owner that are not subject to federal tax law filing requirements, where the required information may not exist or be obtainable by U.S. authorities, and this deficiency should be addressed. Overall, it should be noted that the cases in which these issues arise in practice are small compared with the totality of the United States' information exchange program.

Introduction

Information and methodology used for the peer review of the United States

10.   The assessment of the legal and regulatory framework of the United States and the practical implementation and effectiveness of this framework was based on the international standards for transparency and exchange of information as described in the Global Forum's Terms of Reference, and was prepared using the Global Forum's Methodology for Peer Reviews and Non-Member Reviews. The assessment was based on the laws, regulations, and exchange of information mechanisms in force or effect as at February 2011, other information, explanations and materials supplied by the United States during the on-site visit that took place on 15-17 November, and information supplied by partner jurisdictions. During the on-site visit, the assessment team met with officials and representatives of the relevant US public agencies including the Department of the Treasury and the Internal Revenue Service (see Annex 4).

11.   The Terms of Reference break down the standards of transparency and exchange of information into 10 essential elements and 31 enumerated aspects under three broad categories: (A) availability of information; (B) access to information; and (C) exchanging information. This combined review assesses United States' legal and regulatory framework and the implementation and effectiveness of this framework against these elements and each of the enumerated aspects. In respect of each essential element a determination is made regarding the United States' legal and regulatory framework that either (i) the element is in place, (ii) the element is in place but certain aspects of the legal implementation of the element need improvement, or (iii) the element is not in place. These determinations are accompanied by recommendations for improvement where relevant. In addition, to reflect the Phase 2 component, recommendations are also made concerning the United States' practical application of each of the essential elements. As outlined in the Note on Assessment Criteria, following a jurisdiction's Phase 2 review, a "rating" will be applied to each of the essential elements to reflect the overall

position of a jurisdiction. However this rating will only be published "at such time as a representative subset of Phase 2 reviews is completed". This report therefore includes recommendations in respect of the United States' legal and regulatory framework and the actual implementation of the essential elements, as well as a determination on the legal and regulatory framework, but it does not include a rating of the elements.

12. The assessment was conducted by an assessment team composed of two expert assessors and two representatives of the Global Forum Secretariat: Monica Bhatia, Additional Commissioner of Income Tax, Department of Revenue, Ministry of Finance, Government of India; Roberta Poza Cid, Spanish Ministry of Finance; Dónal Godfrey and Andrew Auerbach from the Global Forum Secretariat.

Overview of the United States

General information on legal system and the taxation system

13. The United States of America (U.S.) is a constitution-based federal republic whose government is divided into executive, legislative, and judicial branches. These branches feature a system of checks and balances, whereby each branch functions with powers sufficient to prevent any one branch from dominating the others. The executive branch is headed by an elected President and Vice-President and an appointed Cabinet that operates through various federal departments and agencies, which in the area of tax administration include the Department of Treasury and its agency, the IRS. The federal legislature, known as Congress, consists of the House of Representatives and the Senate. The House of Representatives numbers 435 total members, allocated among the states commensurate with population. The Senate comprises 100 seats, two per state. The states similarly have legislative bodies. The judicial branch is made up of the U.S. Supreme Court, Federal Courts of Appeal, Federal District Courts, and other federal-level courts such as the U.S. Tax Court. There are also courts on the sub-national level, including state-wide courts and municipal courts. The U.S. has a federal system of government featuring a complex regime of codified and uncodified sources of law at both federal and sub-national levels.

14. At both the federal and state levels, the law of the United States was originally derived largely from the common law system of English law. However, U.S. law has diverged greatly from English law both in terms of substance and procedure, and has incorporated certain features resembling civil law.

15. The U.S. Constitution enumerates the broad areas where the federal government has legislative authority (*e.g.* coining of money, declaring war) and provides that the "Constitution, and the Laws …made in pursuance thereof;

and all treaties made… under the authority of the United States, shall be the supreme Law of the Land." (Art. VI, § 2, known as the "Supremacy Clause"). Congress may "make all laws which shall be necessary and proper" for executing any of its enumerated powers, and the Constitution prohibits the states from exercising certain powers (*e.g.* entering into treaties or coining money). Because of the Supremacy Clause, a federal law may supersede or preempt a state or local law (referred to as the "Preemption Doctrine"). For example, if a state law conflicts with federal law that falls within Congress' authority, the state law will be invalidated. In short, the effect of the Supremacy Clause is that the federal government, in exercising its constitutional powers, will generally prevail over any conflicting or inconsistent exercise of state power.

16.   Under the U.S. Constitution, both laws of the U.S. and treaties are treated as the supreme law of the land. When an act of Congress and a treaty relate to the same subject, the courts will endeavor to construe them so as to give effect to both, if that can be done without violating the language of either. A later-in-time treaty will often be intended to override an earlier statute, and will do so. In the case of a conflict between an earlier treaty and a later statute, the courts do not favor the repudiation of an earlier treaty by implication and require clear indications that Congress, in enacting subsequent inconsistent legislation, meant to supersede the earlier treaty.

System of Taxation

17.   The United States federal system of government results in a multi-tiered system of taxation. The federal government of the United States and the various state and local governments of the United States impose a wide range of taxes and duties. Individual and corporate income tax and payroll tax account for the bulk of federal government revenue. The federal government also imposes estate and gift tax and certain excise taxes. Each of the states imposes various taxes in addition to those imposed by the federal government. Among the common types of taxes that states impose are personal income tax, corporate income tax, sales tax, real property tax, fuel tax, and estate and gift tax.

18.   The federal government taxes U.S. citizens and residents and U.S. corporations on worldwide income annually. Different graduated tax rates apply to individuals and corporations, depending on their taxable net income. The highest federal rate applicable to both individuals and corporations is 35% for the 2010 taxable year.

19.   The United States taxes non-resident individuals and foreign corporations under two systems, both of which are reported on annual tax returns filed with the Internal Revenue Service. First, to the extent that such persons are engaged in the conduct of a trade or business in the United States (a "U.S. trade

or business"), these persons are subject to tax on income effectively connected with the U.S. trade or business ("ECI") at the same graduated rates as resident individuals and U.S. corporations, respectively. The United States also taxes foreign persons on their fixed, determinable, annual or periodical income from U.S. sources (*e.g.* interest, dividends, rents, and royalties) on a gross basis at a 30 percent rate. This gross basis tax is generally collected by withholding of such tax at the time the income is paid, and may be reduced by treaty.

20.   In general, the United States taxes a U.S. shareholder on the active foreign business income earned through a foreign corporation when that income is distributed to the shareholder. However, the United States has special rules requiring a U.S. shareholder to include in income its share of certain income earned by certain foreign corporations, such as "controlled foreign corporations" as well as "passive foreign investment companies," in the year the income is earned, without regard to whether it is distributed. Generally, these special rules focus on income that is highly mobile, such as passive investment income (*e.g.* interest and dividends).

21.   In the United States, trusts and estates are generally taxable entities. However, they generally are allowed a deduction for income that is distributed to beneficiaries in the year it is earned. Beneficiaries take such distributions into income annually. Thus, a trust or estate ordinarily pays no income tax for a year in which it distributes all of its income from that year. Undistributed income is taxable at the rates applicable to an individual. However, the tax brackets are more compressed. For example, for 2010 the top tax rate of 35% applies to a single individual's income in excess of USD 373 650, but to a trust's income in excess of USD 11 200.

22.   The United States taxes income earned by partnerships on a flow-through basis. Thus, income of a partnership is taxed to the partners annually. Certain publicly-traded partnerships are, however, taxed as corporations.

Overview of commercial laws and other relevant factors for exchange of information

State Law

23.   Individual states have the power to promulgate laws relating to the creation, organization, and dissolution of corporations and other legal entities. State corporation laws require that articles of incorporation and by-laws be adopted to document the corporation's creation and to define the rights and obligations of officers, directors, shareholders, and other persons within its structure. States also have registration laws requiring corporations that incorporate in other states (or countries) to register to do in-state business.

24.   With respect to the specific provisions of the various U.S. states' corporation laws, 30 states have adopted in whole or in large part the Model Business Corporation Act (MBCA), developed by the American Bar Association in 1984 and since periodically amended, to encourage uniformity among states. The material in this report is generally based on the MBCA and Delaware law, as representative of the laws of the states generally, although the law in other states is also considered where appropriate. The United States considers that the MBCA and Delaware law as appropriate proxies for other state laws in this respect because of the wide acceptance of the MBCA and the wide use of Delaware as a jurisdiction for corporate formation.

25.   The LLC is a fairly recent business form that is now authorized by the laws of every state. Like a corporation, it protects its owners (referred to as members) from some debts and obligations. For federal income tax purposes an LLC may elect to be taxed either as a corporation or on a pass-through basis in the manner of a partnership. Where the LLC has only one member and is treated as a pass-through entity then it is disregarded as separate from its owner for federal income tax purposes. This results in the assets and liabilities of the LLC being treated as the assets and liabilities of the owner for federal income tax purposes.

Federal Law

26.   As a general matter (and subject to various exceptions), state laws govern the internal affairs of corporations and other legal entities, while federal laws primarily govern matters involving the trading of securities, including requirements for disclosure of information material to the value of such securities. For instance, Congress enacted the Securities Act of 1933, which regulates how publicly-held corporate securities are issued and sold by requiring disclosure of specified information concerning such securities and prohibiting fraud in the offer and sale of such securities.

Overview of factors affecting exchange of information

27.   The United States has for many years had a very active exchange-of-information program, in addition to a very active program of spontaneous and routine information exchange involving millions of items of information each year.

28.   The program relies primarily on the federal income tax information reporting and enforcement architectures of the United States. Under U.S. law, inbound treaty-based requests are placed on the same footing as domestic tax investigations. Beyond tax information reporting and administrative tax enforcement, other elements of the U.S. federal legal framework affecting exchange of information for tax purposes include the regulatory framework

under Title 31 of the United States Code (addressing money-laundering and customer due diligence issues), Title 12 of the Code (providing limitations on financial privacy), and Title 15 of the Code (providing for securities regulation).

Regulation under the Bank Secrecy Act

29.   The Currency and Foreign Transactions Reporting Act, commonly known as the Bank Secrecy Act (BSA), was enacted by the U.S. Congress in 1970 to establish requirements for recordkeeping and reporting by banks and a variety of other financial institutions and businesses and in some cases by individuals. In its capacity as administrator of the BSA, the Financial Crimes Enforcement Network (FinCEN) has authority to examine financial institutions and other businesses for compliance with the BSA but has delegated this examination authority to other federal agencies. In the case of federally regulated financial institutions (banks, securities and futures firms and mutual funds), examination authority has been delegated to the federal regulators for the particular industry. These regulators supervise and examine the financial institutions that they regulate for compliance with applicable laws and regulations, including the BSA and its implementing regulations.

30.   In the case of other businesses subject to the BSA that do not have a federal regulator, FinCEN has delegated examination responsibility to the IRS. FinCEN has retained the authority to propose regulations and assess civil penalties for these businesses.

Anti-money laundering and customer due diligence

31.   The BSA also imposes requirements on banks and other financial institutions to adopt and implement programs to prevent and detect money laundering. Although banks have been required to implement such programs since 1987, the USA PATRIOT Act, enacted in 2001, expanded this requirement so that many additional types of financial institutions, including securities and futures firms, mutual funds, money services businesses (MSBs), and life insurance companies, are required to establish proactive anti-money laundering (AML) programs aimed at protecting their institutions and businesses and, in turn, the U.S. financial system from the risks of money laundering, terrorist financing and other financial crimes (including tax evasion).

Overview of the financial sector and relevant professions

32.   A variety of types of financial institutions and businesses are involved in the U.S. financial system. Financial institutions and businesses may be subject to supervision and examination by a number of regulatory

agencies, both federal and state, and the same institution or business may be regulated for different purposes by more than one regulator.

Banking sector

33.   Depository institutions in the U.S. may be chartered at either the national or the state level and may be involved in many activities, including the following: safeguarding money and valuables; providing loans and credit; offering payment services, such as checking accounts, money orders, and cashier's checks; and dealing in and holding Treasury and agency debt securities. Depository institutions also may affiliate more broadly with securities and insurance underwriters. Commercial banks in the U.S. offer a full range of services for individuals, businesses, and governments and range in size from global banks to regional and community banks.

Federal regulation

34.   Depending on a banking organization's charter and organizational structure, it may be subject to several federal and state banking regulators. Banks, savings and loan associations, and credit unions are generally supervised by at least one of the five federal bank regulatory agencies – the Board of Governors of the Federal Reserve System (Federal Reserve), the Office of the Comptroller of the Currency (OCC), the Federal Deposit Insurance Corporation (FDIC), the Office of Thrift Supervision (OTS), or the National Credit Union Administration (NCUA). Due to its role as the provider of deposit insurance, the FDIC also supervises banks that are primarily overseen by the OCC, the Federal Reserve, or the OTS.

State regulation

35.   State regulators charter and license a large number of banks, savings associations, and credit unions, as well as many money services businesses, and share oversight responsibility with the relevant federal agencies. For example, a California state bank that is not a member of the Federal Reserve System would be regulated by both the California Department of Financial Institutions and the FDIC.

Securities and futures sector

36.   Brokerage firms may be operated as full-service, limited service, or discount, and may offer many or all of their services online. Full-service brokers help clients develop an investment portfolio, manage their investments, or make recommendations regarding which investments to buy. Discount firms often do not offer advice about specific securities, although they may

provide third party analysis, sometimes for a fee. Purely online brokerage firms offer their services over the Internet in order to help reduce costs. Brokerage firms also provide investment-banking services (*i.e.* they act as intermediaries between companies and governments that would like to raise money and those with money or capital to invest). Investment bankers also advise businesses on merger and acquisition strategies.

37.   Companies that specialize in providing investment advice, portfolio management, and trust, fiduciary, and custody activities are also part of the securities sector. These companies range from very large mutual fund management companies to self-employed personal financial advisers or financial planners. As of 31 December 2009, there were 5253 broker-dealers registered with the SEC, of which more than 4 600 do business with the public.

38.   Equity securities are primarily traded on registered securities exchanges, like the New York Stock Exchange (NYSE) and the NASDAQ, and to a much lesser extent on over-the-counter markets (OTC markets). As of 31 December 2009, there were 14 registered securities exchanges.

39.   Mutual funds, which are also known as open-end registered investment companies, closed-end investment companies, and Unit Investment Trusts (UITs), are popular investment vehicles in the U.S. As of July 2010, there were 7 500 mutual funds with assets of USD 10.9 trillion, 624 closed-end funds with assets of USD 227.3 billion, and over 6 019 UITs with a value of USD 38.3 billion. Investment advisers manage assets of investors, both on an individual and on a pooled account basis. As of July 2010, there were more than 11 000 investment advisers registered with the SEC. Collectively, those registered investment advisers managed USD 38 trillion in assets, including assets of the managed investment companies described earlier.

Securities and futures regulation

40.   The U.S. Securities and Exchange Commission (SEC) is the federal regulator of the securities markets and many market participants. The SEC administers the federal securities laws, and adopts rules implementing those laws. The SEC's statutory enforcement authority allows it to bring civil enforcement actions against individuals or companies alleged to have committed accounting fraud, provided false information, or engaged in insider trading or other violations of the securities law. The SEC also works in parallel with criminal law enforcement agencies to prosecute individuals and companies alike for offenses which include a criminal violation.

Recent developments

41.   In 2010, the United States took a number of steps to further strengthen the extensive information reporting and associated enforcement regimes that help ensure compliance with the U.S. tax system and the U.S. AML/KYC regime.

42.   Any legal entity that opens an account with a financial institution in the United States must, among other requirements, obtain an Employer Identification Number (EIN) from the IRS (as must any legal entity with employees, any legal entity with a qualified retirement plan, and any legal entity that is required to file a tax return for employment taxes, excise taxes, or income taxes). The IRS application for an EIN was revised in January 2010 to specifically preclude the identification of a nominee individual, and instead requires the identification of a "responsible party." Notably, the revised form and instructions define the "responsible party" as the owner of the entity in the case of an entity that is disregarded as separate from its owner for tax purposes (*e.g.* single-member LLCs), for entities with shares or interests traded on a public exchange, or which are registered with the Securities and Exchange Commission. For all other entities, "responsible party" is the person who has a level of control over, or entitlement to, the funds or assets in the entity that, as a practical matter, enables the individual directly or indirectly, to control, manage, or direct the entity and the disposition of its funds and assets.

43.   On February 26, 2010, the Treasury Department's Financial Crimes Enforcement Network (FinCEN) issued a Notice of Proposed Rulemaking to revise the longstanding regulations implementing the provision of the Bank Secrecy Act (BSA) regarding reporting of foreign financial accounts. The current regulations implementing 31 U.S.C. § 5314 provide that each person subject to the jurisdiction of the United States having a financial interest in, or signature or other authority over, a bank, securities, or other financial account in a foreign country has an obligation to "report such relationship to the Commissioner of Internal Revenue for each year in which such relationship exists, and … provide such information as shall be specified in a reporting form prescribed by the Secretary to be filed by such persons." 31 C.F.R. § 103.24. 31 C.F.R. § 103.27 requires the form to be filed with respect to foreign financial accounts exceeding USD 10 000. Records of accounts are required to be reported to the Treasury Department for each person having a financial interest in or signature or other authority over such an account. 31 C.F.R. § 103.32. Such persons include, among others, U.S. trustees of trusts (regardless of whether the trust is formed under domestic or foreign law). The records must be maintained for a period of five years.

44.   The form used to file the report required by 31 C.F.R. § 103.24 is the Report of Foreign Bank and Financial Accounts – Form TD F 90-22.1 (the

FBAR). FinCEN's proposed regulations would amend 31 C.F.R. § 103.24 by using a new term "United States person" to indicate persons required to file an FBAR. Under the proposed rulemaking a United States person is defined as a citizen or resident of the United States, or an entity, including but not limited to a corporation, partnership, trust or limited liability company, created, organized, or formed under the laws of the United States, any state, the District of Columbia, or the Territories and Insular Possessions of the United States.

45.   The instructions included in the proposed regulations clarify that the definition of "United States person" for these purposes applies to an entity regardless of whether the entity is disregarded for federal income tax purposes. Thus, under the proposed regulations a limited liability company organized in any state of the United States that has a foreign financial account will be required to file an FBAR annually. An LLC will be required to provide an employer identification number (EIN) as part of the FBAR filing if it has one. In the case of an LLC that does not have an EIN, item 4 of the proposed FBAR instructions would require the filer to provide information from an official foreign government document that would, inter alia, identify the filer and verify the filer's nationality or residence, although it is not clear what foreign government document would apply to an LLC organized under the laws of one of the states in these circumstances. The proposed regulations also clarify the meaning of "a bank, securities, or other financial account" so as to ensure that it has comprehensive application to a very wide range of financial accounts.[1] The civil penalty for willfully failing to disclose a foreign financial account on an FBAR is the greater of USD 100 000 or 50% of the balance in the account at the time of the violation. The criminal penalty for willfully failing to report a foreign financial account on an FBAR includes a maximum fine of USD 250 000, a maximum term of imprisonment of five years, or both, with even higher penalties in certain circumstances.[2]

---

1.   For example, "other financial account" would include an account with a person that is in the business of accepting deposits as a financial agency; an account that is an insurance policy with a cash value or an annuity policy; an account with a person that acts as a broker or dealer for futures or options transactions in any commodity on or subject to the rules of a commodity exchange or association; or an account with a mutual fund or similar pooled fund issuing shares that are available to the general public and that have a regular net asset value determination and regular redemptions.

2.   This report represents the state of U.S. law as of January 2011. On 23 February 2011, the U.S. Treasury's Financial Crimes Enforcement Network (FinCEN) issued a final rule to amend the Bank Secrecy Act (BSA) regulations regarding reports of foreign financial accounts in line with the Notice of Proposed Rulemaking. The new rules are effective March 28, 2011.

46.   On March 18, 2010, the Hiring Incentives to Restore Employment Act of 2010, Pub. L. 111-147 (H.R. 2847) (the HIRE Act), was enacted into law. Section 501(a) of the Act added a new chapter 4 (I.R.C. §§ 1471 – 1474) to Subtitle A of the Internal Revenue Code. Chapter 4 originally appeared as part of the Foreign Account Tax Compliance Act, and therefore is sometimes referred to as "FATCA." Chapter 4 is generally effective beginning after December 31, 2012. Chapter 4 expands the information reporting require-ments to which certain foreign financial institutions (FFIs) are subject and requires them to: (i) obtain such information regarding each holder of each account maintained by the FFI as is necessary to determine which (if any) of such accounts are U.S. accounts; (ii) comply with due diligence procedures the Secretary may require with respect to the identification of U.S. accounts; and (iii) report certain information with respect to U.S. accounts maintained by the FFI. I.R.C. § 1471(b) and (c). [U.S. accounts for this purpose are financial accounts that are held by one or more specified U.S. persons or U.S.-owned foreign entities. A specified U.S. person is (except as otherwise provided by the Secretary) any United States person other than certain types of entities that are expressly excluded under I.R.C. section 1473(3). Thus, unless a U.S. legal entity is in a class of persons specifically excluded by the statute or another exception applies, certain foreign financial institutions are statutorily required to report information to the IRS regarding the foreign accounts of that entity. Such information includes the account number, the account balance or value, and, to the extent provided by the Secretary of the Treasury, the gross receipts and gross withdrawals or payments from the account (determined for such period and in such manner as the Secretary of the Treasury may provide). I.R.C. § 1471(c).

47.   In addition to the incentives for foreign financial institutions to assist the IRS in collecting information intended to prevent offshore tax evasion, the HIRE Act also includes offshore compliance provisions that, among other noteworthy items, increase reporting and increase penalties for failing to report on certain foreign trusts, and require each person that is a shareholder of a passive foreign investment company to file an annual information return containing certain information.

48.   On January 6, 2011, the U.S. Treasury published proposed regula-tions that would require the automatic information reporting to the IRS of bank deposit interest paid with respect to accounts maintained by financial institutions at offices within the United States of all individuals not resident in the United States. This rule also would require that institutions prepare and deliver a statement to nonresident individuals to the effect that the informa-tion being furnished by the financial institution to the IRS may be furnished to the government of the foreign country where the recipient resides.

Compliance with the Standards

A. Availability of Information

Overview

49. Effective exchange of information requires the availability of reliable information. In particular it requires information on the identity of owners and other stakeholders as well as information on the transactions carried out by entities and other organisational structures. Such information may be kept for tax, regulatory, commercial or other reasons. If such information is not kept or the information is not maintained for a reasonable period of time, a jurisdiction's competent authority may not be able to obtain and provide it when requested. This section of the report describes and assesses the United States' legal and regulatory framework on availability of information. It also assesses the implementation and effectiveness of this framework.

50. The legal and regulatory framework is generally in place for all entities and arrangements to maintain ownership and identity information through the application of the United States' various tax law provisions as well as applicable state law. Corporations are generally required to maintain a register of owners under state law. Any partnership formed under U.S. law that has income, credits or deductions for U.S. tax purposes will be required to file an income tax return in which all of its partners are identified. However, limited liability companies that have only one owner may be disregarded for U.S. federal income tax purposes, and if such an entity is disregarded for federal income tax purposes, has no income that is effectively connected with the conduct of a trade or business in the United States, no

U.S. owner, no other U.S. source income, no employees in the United States, no other activity in the United States, and no other reason that the entity is subject to federal income taxes, employment taxes, or excise taxes, then information on its owner will not be available pursuant to U.S. federal tax laws. Information may be held in accordance with the law of the state of the entity's formation, though this is not guaranteed in all cases.

51.   Information concerning trustees, settlors and beneficiaries of trusts that are subject to federal income tax law, anti-money laundering law or state law is available. Trusts that are treated as foreign trusts for U.S. federal income tax purposes, but that have a U.S. resident trustee may often be subject to state law requirements to know the settlors, trustees and beneficiaries of a trust, whether or not the trust is governed by foreign law. There may be limited circumstances where a trustee resident in the United States that is the trustee of a non-U.S. trust is not subject to any U.S. rules requiring the maintenance of such information. The trustee would be subject to the jurisdiction of a U.S. court and the IRS summons power, and would be required to file an FBAR. As a practical matter, the availability of information on trusts has not posed any problems for exchange of information purposes.

52.   Corporations and partnerships must provide the IRS annually a balance sheet that agrees with their books and records, as well as a schedule that reconciles their income statement per their books of account with their income statement per their tax return. Generally, trustees of trusts must maintain detailed accounting information pursuant to federal tax law, state statutory law, and case law. There may be limited circumstances where a trustee resident in the United States that is the trustee of a non-U.S. trust is not subject to any U.S. rules requiring the maintenance of such information, although the trustee would be required to file an FBAR. The requirements to maintain underlying records for accounting information for a minimum of 5 years is not expressly provided for under federal law in all cases. The generally applicable rules under federal tax law further contain a statute of limitations rule that all taxpayers must maintain records so long as they may be relevant for the determination of federal income tax. This period may be anywhere from just over 3 years to an indefinite period (for example, in the case of corporations the calculation of earnings and profits may depend on all transactions undertaken throughout the corporation's lifetime). There is no penalty for failing to maintain records, but a taxpayer who is not able to support their tax position will be unable to rebut a re-assessment by the IRS. In addition, where an entity is disregarded for federal tax purposes, and is not otherwise subject to tax filing requirements, this rule will not apply. Specific additional rules under the federal tax law, other federal law or state law apply in certain cases.

53.   Anti-money laundering law as well as applicable banking regulations ensure that bank information is available.

A.1. Ownership and identity information

> Jurisdictions should ensure that ownership and identity information for all relevant entities and arrangements is available to their competent authorities.

Companies (ToR³ A.1.1)

54. Legal entities generally are created under the laws of one of the several states. Each of the states allows for the creation of corporations. In general, a corporation is a legal entity that is capitalized by share contributions and whose owners' liability for the corporation's obligations is limited to the amount of their contributions.

55. Historically, the corporation has been the dominant business form in the United States. In recent years the LLC has become increasingly popular. This is a relatively new business form that shares certain features of a corporation and certain features of a partnership. Like the corporation it protects its owners (referred to as members) from some debts and obligations. Wyoming passed the first law permitting formation of LLCs in 1977. All 50 states now allow for the formation of LLCs.

56. State laws regarding the formation of an LLC tend to reflect an interest in allowing greater contractual flexibility among the owners than do the rules governing the formation of corporations. The income of LLCs with more than one member is generally not taxed directly, but as with partnerships, is passed through to the owners to the extent the LLC does not elect to be taxed as a corporation. For that reason, LLCs will be discussed in Section A1.3 (Partnerships). For federal tax purposes, an LLC with only one member is disregarded as an entity separate from its member, unless it makes an affirmative election to be classified as a corporation. Where the LLC is disregarded then the owner is treated as owning the LLC's assets directly. Whether an organization is treated as an entity separate from its owners for federal tax law purposes is a matter of federal tax law and does not depend on whether the organization is recognized as an entity under state law. Treas. Reg. § 301.7701-1.

57. The figure below includes information on the number of corporations and LLCs formed in the top five states in 2009 along with information on corporate and LLC formation in Nevada and Wyoming. New York had the largest number of corporations on file followed by Pennsylvania, Florida, California and Texas. Delaware had the largest number of LLCs followed by Florida, California, New York and Texas. The numbers of incorporations in Nevada and Wyoming, popularly considered as significant centres for corporate formation, are small by comparison to the five biggest states.

---

3. Terms of Reference to Monitor and Review Progress Towards Transparency and Exchange of Information

Figure 1. Number of Corporations and LLCs formed in Selected States in 2009

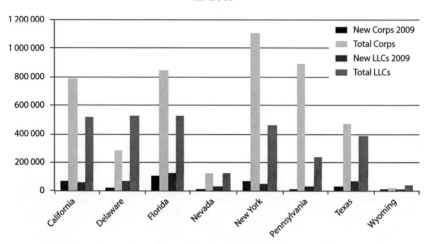

Source: International Association of Commercial Administrators – Annual Jurisdictional Report (available at *www.iaca.org/iacareg/ARJDisplay.php?year=2009*).

58.   If a corporation with a single class of stock has no more than 100 shareholders, none of whom are non-resident aliens or entities (other than certain tax-exempt organizations and certain estates and trusts), the corporation generally may elect to be taxed as a pass-through entity under subchapter S of the Internal Revenue Code (a so-called S corporation).

59.   See Section A2 (Partnerships) for a discussion of partnerships, S corporations and LLCs to the extent an LLC does not elect to be taxed as a corporation.

Ownership and identity information held by corporations

60.   Under Delaware law and the Model Business Corporation Act, 4th Edition, 2007 (MBCA), a corporation is formed upon filing articles of incorporation with the relevant governmental office in the relevant state. The articles set forth the name and address of the incorporator as well as provide the name, address and phone number of a natural person authorised to receive process. Under the Model Business Corporation Act, every corporation must maintain "a record of its shareholders, in a form that permits preparation of a list of the names and addresses of all shareholders in alphabetical order by class of shares showing the number and class of shares held by each" (MBCA § 16.01(c)). Under Delaware law, a corporation is required to produce, at the request of any stockholder, the corporation's stock ledger and a list of its

stockholders (DGCL § 220). The requirement to maintain a record of share-holders or a stock ledger applies regardless of the residence of the shareholder or stockholder (the terms are synonymous – both refer to an equity inter-est in the body corporate) and is separate and distinct from any obligation to maintain information for U.S. federal income tax purposes. It should be noted, however, that corporations, unlike LLCs, are not eligible to be treated as a pass-through for U.S. federal income tax purposes, and so are in all cases taxed as corporations as described in the next section Ownership and Identity Information provided to Government Authorities – Federal Tax Law.

61.   Similar or equivalent provisions are included in the New York Business Corporations Law 2001 and the Pennsylvania Corporations and Unincorporated Associations Law. In California a record of shares is required to be maintained by or on behalf of the corporation while in Florida a corpo-ration or its agent must maintain "a record of its shareholders in a form that permits preparation of a list of the names and addresses of all shareholders in alphabetical order by class of shares showing the number and series of shares held by each" (Florida Business Corporations Act Sec. 607.1601).

62.   The U.S. imposes comprehensive reporting requirements at the fed-eral level for companies that offer securities to the public, or whose securities are listed on a U.S. stock exchange. The U.S. federal securities laws require the reporting of beneficial ownership by persons who beneficially own or are deemed to beneficially own more than 5% of a voting class of a company's equity securities that, with limited exception, is registered under Section 12 of the Securities Exchange Act of 1934. This includes U.S. and foreign issu-ers that list their stock for trading on a U.S. stock exchange. These reports are required to be filed under Sections 13(d) and (g) of the Exchange Act, and publicly disclose the identity of the filer(s), the amount of the holdings, and, in some cases, any plans or proposals the filer may have with respect to the company. For companies with a class of equity securities registered under Section 12, Section 16 of the Exchange Act imposes a separate reporting obligation on officers, directors, and more than 10% beneficial owners to file public reports of their transactions and holdings in the company's securities. Securities registered by a foreign private issuer, however, are exempted from Section 16. U.S. and foreign companies that offer securities for public invest-ment generally also are required to disclose in their annual reports, proxy or information statements, and securities offering registration statements, the identity and amount of shares held by any beneficial owner of more than 5% of a voting class of equity securities, regardless of whether those securities are registered under Section 12, as well as the amount of equity securities beneficially owned by the directors and executive officers.

63.   Pursuant to I.R.C section 6001, every taxpayer, including U.S. com-panies whether or not publicly traded, must keep books and records sufficient

to establish amounts reported in a tax return. These books and records include the books and records required to satisfy the reporting requirements described below including ownership reporting per se and reporting with respect to payments made to owners (notably including dividend payments and, in the case of owners that are not U.S. persons, reporting with respect to all fixed, determinable, annual, or periodical gains, profit, or income).

Ownership and identity information provided to government authorities – Federal Tax Law

64.   Any corporation formed under U.S. law must apply for an Employer Identification Number (EIN) from the IRS under I.R.C. section 6109 if it:

- Has employees,

- Has a qualified retirement plan, or

- Is required to file tax returns for:

- Employment taxes,

  - Excise taxes, or

  - Income taxes

65.   EINs are obtained by filing Form SS-4 with the IRS. This form requires that information concerning the principal officer of the corporation must be provided. It does not ask for shareholder information, however, the application form was amended in January 2010 to specifically preclude the identification of a nominee individual, and instead requires the identification of a "responsible party." For this purpose, the "responsible party" is defined as follows: for entities with shares or interests traded on a public exchange, or which are registered with the Securities and Exchange Commission, "responsible party" is (a) the principal officer, if the business is a corporation, (b) a general partner, if a partnership, (c) the owner of an entity that is disregarded as separate from its owner, *e.g.* single-member LLCs, or (d) a grantor, owner, or trustee if a trust. For all other entities, "responsible party" is the person who has a level of control over, or entitlement to, the funds or assets in the entity that, as a practical matter, enables the individual, directly or indirectly, to control, manage or direct the entity and the disposition of its funds. Once an EIN has been obtained, there is no need to update the EIN to take account of any change in circumstances.

66.   On an annual basis, certain ownership information is reported as part of the income tax return that corporations subject to tax are required to file under I.R.C. section 6012(a)(2). In particular, corporations must report the identity of any person that owns (directly) at least 20% or (directly

or indirectly) at least 50% of the total voting power of the corporation. Furthermore, the corporation must report whether any foreign person owns, directly or indirectly, at least 25% of the corporation (by vote or value). The Form 1120 also provides the identity and ownership information, including compensation, of all corporate officers. (IRS Form 1120 Schedule E).

67. Corporations organised in the United States that are owned more than 25%, directly or indirectly, by foreign persons are "reporting corporations" subject to the additional information reporting requirements under I.R.C. section 6038A. Reporting corporations must file an annual information return (Form 5472) detailing, with respect to each direct 25% foreign shareholder, each ultimate indirect 25% foreign shareholder, and each related party with which the reporting corporation had any transaction during the year, the following identifying information: name; address; identification number; principal countries where business is conducted; and country of citizenship, organization or incorporation. Form 5472 also requires a description of all monetary and non-monetary transactions between the reporting corporation and any foreign related party, and its principal business activity, relationship, and principal countries where business is conducted.

68. Any corporation that is formed under domestic law (and any LLC or other legal entity taxed as a corporation under federal law) and makes payments of dividends aggregating more than USD 10 in any year is required to make a return of such amounts on Form 1099-DIV setting forth the aggregate amount of such payments and the name and address of each person to whom such payments are made (I.R.C. § 6042).

69. A separate set of ownership reporting requirements apply in connection with any amount paid to a foreign person (I.R.C. §§ 1441 through 1464 and the regulations thereunder). Under these rules, the beneficial owner generally is required to be identified, and the payee's status documented. Specifically, a foreign person who is the beneficial owner of dividends, interest, or other fixed or determinable annual or periodical gains, profits, or income from a corporation must complete a Form W-8BEN, Certificate of Foreign Status of Beneficial Owner for United States Tax Withholding. A foreign person who is the beneficial owner of income that is effectively connected with a United States trade or business must provide, Form W-8ECI, Certificate of Foreign Person's Claim that Income is Effectively Connected With the Conduct of a Trade or Business in the United States, to the payor or withholding agent of the effectively connected income. The W-8 forms call for identification of the beneficial owner by name, residence address, mailing address, country, type of entity (if applicable), and EIN or other taxpayer identification number. Failure to provide this beneficial ownership information in order to establish that the beneficial owner is eligible for an exemption from withholding, or a reduced rate of withholding under an income tax

treaty, generally results in a 30% withholding tax imposed on payments of fixed, determinable, annual, or periodical gains, profits, or income made to the legal owner of the payment.

Foreign corporations

70.   Foreign corporations that are engaged in a U.S. trade or business are required to obtain an EIN and file tax returns. The rules described above regarding the reporting of ownership details in the Form 1120 will therefore apply. In particular, corporations must report the identity of any person that owns (directly) at least 20% or (directly or indirectly) at least 50% of the total voting power of the corporation. Furthermore, the corporation must report whether any foreign person owns, directly or indirectly, at least 25% of the corporation (by vote or value) (IRS Form 1120-F).

71.   Foreign corporations engaged in a U.S. trade or business are specifically required to furnish and maintain records relating to each person which is a related party to the corporation and which had any transaction with the reporting corporation during its taxable year, the manner in which the foreign corporation is related to the person, and information related to any transactions between the foreign corporation and any related party. A transaction would include any payment to or contribution of value from a shareholder. Related party for these purposes includes any non-US person that owns 25% of the vote or value of the corporation. Regulations provide a safe harbour specifying what documents will satisfy this record-keeping requirement. These safe harbour documents include records relating to the ownership and capital structure of the foreign corporation, including a worldwide organisation chart. (IRC §6038C, 6038A and regulations issued thereunder).

72.   The concept of being "engaged in a U.S. trade or business" for U.S. federal income tax purposes is very broad, and may include circumstances where a foreign person has only completed isolated transactions in the United States. Consequently, a great deal of ownership information may be available for many corporations that have, for the purposes of the *Terms of Reference*, only a slight connection with the United States.

Nominees

73.   Through the federal tax system, nominees generally are required to have and provide information regarding the identity of the person on whose behalf the shares are held.

74.   Chapter 61 of the Internal Revenue Code provides a comprehensive information reporting regime for tax purposes. I.R.C. section 6041(a) provides that persons engaged in a trade or business and making payment in the

course of such trade or business to another person, of rent, salaries, or other fixed or determinable gains, profits and income of USD 600 or more in any taxable year must file an information return showing the name and address of the recipient of such payment. I.R.C. section 6042(a)(1) provides that every person who pays dividends of USD 10 or more to any other person during any calendar year, or who receives payments of dividends as a nominee and who makes such payments to any other person with respect to the dividends so received must file an information return stating the name and address of the ultimate recipient. I.R.C. section 6045 generally requires stockbrokers and companies closing real estate transactions to file similar information returns with respect to gross proceeds of transactions. I.R.C. section 6049 provides similar rules with respect to payments of interest. In 2009, more than 3 billion information returns were filed with the IRS.

75.   The Treasury Regulations under such Internal Revenue Code sections prescribe Form 1099 as the basic official form on which to file such information returns. The regulations further provide that every person acting as a nominee shall file such a return identifying the person on behalf of whom the payment was received. Treas. Reg. §§ 301.6042-2(a)(1)(i), 1.6049-4(b)(3)(i), 1.6049-4(f)(4).

76.   The General Instructions to Form 1099 implement these requirements by providing that a person receiving Form 1099 for amounts that actually belong to another person is considered a nominee recipient and must file the same type of Form 1099 for such beneficial owner, identifying the beneficial owner and showing the portion of the income allocable to that owner.

77.   If there is more than one level of nominee in a chain of ownership, these information reporting requirements would apply successively to each nominee, so that the ultimate nominee would be required to have and provide information regarding the identity of the ultimate owner. Where a person having control, receipt, custody, disposal, or payment of any item of dividends, rents, salaries, wages, premiums, annuities, compensations, remunerations, emoluments, or other fixed or determinable annual or periodical gains, profits, or income (FDAP) makes payments to a non-resident alien, another information reporting regime (Chapter 3 of the Internal Revenue Code) applies. Payments made to foreign nominees are covered by the Chapter 3 information reporting regime, which is reinforced with a 30% withholding tax.

78.   A foreign person who is the beneficial owner of income subject to Chapter 3 withholding must provide one of three varieties of W-8 forms to the payor of the income. The W-8 forms call for identification of the beneficial owner by name, residence address, mailing address, country of organization, type of entity (if applicable), and EIN or other taxpayer identification number. A foreign person who is an intermediary (including nominee) for the beneficial owner instead must provide Form W-8IMY. The Form W-8IMY

generally requires an intermediary to identify the person(s) for whom the intermediary is receiving the payment by virtue of the fact that it must be accompanied by one of the three other Forms W-8, as applicable.

79.   Ownership information for entities treated as corporations for federal income tax purposes is generally available through a combination of federal and state law, including where held by a nominee. There are extensive reporting obligations that attach to the payment of dividends, particularly when paid to non-U.S. residents.

80.   In practice, peers have not indicated that obtaining ownership information for companies taxed as corporations for federal income tax purposes has been a problem.

Bearer shares (ToR A.1.2)

81.   All 50 states prohibit the issuance of bearer shares. In 2007, Nevada and Wyoming passed legislation prohibiting bearer shares, thereby extending the prohibition to all 50 states.

Anti money laundering law

82.   While the United States anti-money laundering laws and regulations generally emphasize the need for a risk-based approach to customer identification they specifically require that, as part of its customer identification program (CIP), a financial institution must collect (at a minimum) the following identifying information about a customer at the time the customer seeks to open the account: (1) name; (2) for individuals, date of birth; (3) for individuals, a residential or business street address, or, if there is no street address available, an Army Post Office or Fleet Post Office box number or the street address of next of kin or of another contact individual; or, for persons other than individuals, the principal place of business, local office or other physical location; and (4) for U.S. persons, a U.S. taxpayer identification number; or, for non-U.S. persons, one or more of the following: a U.S. taxpayer identification number, passport number and country of issuance; alien identification card number, or number and country of issuance of any other government-issued document evidencing nationality or residence and bearing a photograph or similar safeguard. In addition, the CIP must contain risk-based procedures for verifying each customer's identity. See *e.g.* 31 C.F.R. § 103.121 (for banks), 31 § C.F.R. 103.122 (for broker-dealers); 31 C.F.R. § 103.123 (for FCMs); and 31 C.F.R. § 103.131 (for mutual funds).

83.   For purposes of (4), a "U.S. person" includes both natural persons and legal entities formed in the United States. Thus, any legal entity that opens an account with a financial institution covered by the CIP rules must obtain an

Employer Identification Number from the IRS. The CIP rules apply to banks (including insured banks, commercial banks or trust companies, private bankers, agencies or branches of foreign banks in the United States, credit unions and thrift institutions, securities broker-dealers, futures commission merchants and mutual funds).[4]

84.   Based on a bank's risk assessment of a new account opened by a customer that is not an individual, a bank may need to take additional steps to verify the customer's identity. In addition, the financial institution may need to look through the customer to determine the beneficial owner of the account in connection with the customer due diligence procedures required under other provisions of its BSA compliance program as described in the following section. This would typically be required in the cases of certain trusts, shell entities, and private investment companies, among others.

85.   However, the anti-money laundering laws in the United States do not currently cover company service providers – including resident agents in the case of LLCs. Similarly trust service providers other than banks, trust companies and other financial institutions as described above are not within the scope of the U.S. anti-money laundering rules. The U.S. considers that, in general, the business of providing trust services is limited to banks and trust companies.

Partnerships (ToR A.1.3)

86.   All states allow for the creation of general partnerships and limited partnerships. In addition, as noted above, limited liability companies – while bodies corporate for state law purposes – are generally treated as partnerships for federal income tax purposes and combine both corporate and partnership features and so are dealt with for the purposes of this report under the heading of partnerships. Additionally, many states allow for the creation of limited liability partnerships ("LLPs"), which are a type of general partnership that

---

4.   Financial institutions which do not typically maintain account relationships with their customers, such as money transmitters, check cashers, and money order sellers, are subject to other identification rules that require them to obtain identifying information before conducting a transaction. See, *e.g.* 31 CFR 103.28 which, in the case of transactions involving more than USD 10 000 in currency, requires a financial institution to verify and record the name and address of the individual presenting the transaction, as well as record the identity and taxpayer identification number of any person or entity on whose behalf the transaction is effected; and 31 CFR 103.29 which, in the case of purchases of cashier's checks, money orders and traveler's checks for USD 3 000 or more in currency, requires a financial institution to record indentifying information about the purchaser (*i.e.* name, address, social security number or alien identification number, and date of birth) and verify the purchaser's name and address.

insulates its partners from liability for another partner's actions and obligations, although not from the individual partner's own actions. LLPs tend to be used primarily by professional service firms, particularly those prohibited by State law from organizing as LLCs.

Ownership information provided to government authorities – State Law

87.   Partnerships, other than general partnerships, are required to file their formation document with the relevant governmental authority (typically the relevant state's Secretary of State) in which the partnership is formed. Both the Uniform Limited Partnership Act (2001) (ULPA) section 201 and Delaware Limited Partnership Act (DLPA) in section 17-201, require a certificate to be filed with the relevant governmental authority. To date Alabama, Arkansas, California, Florida, Hawaii, Idaho, Illinois, Iowa, Kentucky, Maine, Minnesota, Nevada, New Mexico, North Dakota, Oklahoma, Washington have adopted the ULPA. The contents of this certificate would typically identify the legal general partners by name and address, and failure to comply with this requirement could result in the partnership's being treated as a general partnership. The ULPA (§210) requires an annual report to be filed after the initial registration in order to keep their limited partnership status current.

88.   New York limited partnership law requires that the partnership maintain a current list of the full name and last known mailing address of each partner (2006 New York Code § 121-106). In Texas and Pennsylvania, a limited partner only becomes a limited partner once the person's admission as a limited partner is reflected in the records of the limited partnership (Texas Business Organizations Code, ch. 153, title 4, sec. 153.101 and Pennsylvania Statutes Title 15, § 8521) and the partnership is required to maintain a list of its limited partners (Business Organizations Code, ch. 153, title 4, sec. 153.551 and Pennsylvania Statutes, Title 15, § 8507).

89.   LLCs (which for the most part are treated as partnerships for federal income tax purposes) generally are formed upon filing a certificate of formation or organization with the Secretary of State in the relevant state. See Revised Uniform Limited Liability Company Act (2006) (ULLCA) § 201; Delaware Limited Liability Company Act (DLLCA) § 18-201. The ULLCA requires the filing of an annual report with the Secretary of State. ULLCA § 209. Typically, there is no requirement to provide details of ownership information on formation of an LLC. Articles of incorporation or organisation must be provided but these are generally not required to contain ownership information, although some states do require some ownership information. Most states also require LLCs to file periodic reports but with some exceptions these generally do not include ownership information.

Federal Tax Law

90.   Under U.S. federal tax law, partnerships are generally treated as pass through entities that are not subject to federal income tax at the entity level. Partners of a partnership are subject to current tax on their distributive shares of the partnership's income, loss, deduction or credit regardless of whether the partnership makes any distributions. An LLC with more than one member is generally classified as a partnership for federal income tax purposes, and an LLC with one member is generally disregarded as an entity separate from the member for federal income tax purposes.

91.   Entities treated as partnerships for U.S. federal income tax purposes created or organized under U.S. law – whether it is a an LLC that is taxed as a partnership, or a general partnership, limited partnership or limited liability partnership – are required both to register with the IRS and to file annual returns, without regard to whether they have US members or US income. Similarly, entities treated as partnerships for U.S. tax purposes (whether domestic or foreign) that earn U.S. source income or income effectively connected with the conduct of a U.S. trade or business are generally required to both register with the IRS and to file annual returns.

92.   An upfront registration requirement applies to partnerships and LLCs at Federal level in that they are among the legal persons or arrangements required to obtain EINs (see above under *Ownership and Identity Information provided to Government Authorities – Federal Tax Law*). The EIN requirement applies even to a single member LLC that is otherwise disregarded as separate from its individual owner for tax purposes.

93.   On an annual basis, ownership information is reported as part of the standard annual return that all U.S. partnerships (including LLCs classified as partnerships) that have income, deductions or credits for tax purposes are required to file under I.R.C. section 6031. This filing is made on Form 1065, U.S. Return of Partnership Income. The partners of a partnership (or members of an LLC taxed as a partnership) are identified in Form 1065. Specifically, as part of the regime whereby each partner reports and pays tax on a distributive share of the partnership's income, loss, deduction, or credit, the partnership must file with Form 1065 a Schedule K-1, Partner's Share of Income, Credits, Deductions, and Other Items, with respect to each partner. Schedule K-1 indicates the name, address, EIN, capital account data, and profit and loss percentages of the partner.

94.   An LLC classified as a partnership for U.S. federal tax purposes would report this same information on Schedules K-1 with respect to the members of the LLC. Form 1065 also requires (on Schedule B-1) reporting on the ownership interest held, directly or indirectly, by any partnership, corporation, LLC, trust, tax-exempt organization, individual or estate that owns, directly or indirectly, an interest of 50% or more in the profit, loss, or capital of the partnership.

95.   A U.S. or foreign partnership that has effectively connected taxable income and foreign partners is required to prepare Form 8805, Foreign Partner's Information Statement of Section 1446 Withholding Tax, on or before the due date of the partnership's federal income tax returns. Treas. Reg. § 1.1446-3(d)(1)(iii). Form 8805 includes the name, address and a required U.S. taxpayer identification number for each foreign partner of the partnership.

Foreign partnerships

96.   Foreign partnerships that earn income effectively connected with the conduct of a trade or business within the U.S. or fixed, determinable, annual, or periodical gains, profits or income are generally subject to the same registration requirement as domestic partnerships. Under I.R.C. section 6109, virtually all legal persons must obtain a federal Employer Identification Number (EIN) from the IRS. Information on the partnership and its general partner must be provided on the application for an EIN (Form SS-4).

97.   Foreign partnerships are also generally subject to the requirement to file an annual return on Form 1065 for any year in which the partnership has gross income derived from sources within the United States or gross income that is effectively connected with the conduct of a trade or business within the United States. I.R.C. § 6031(e). This requirement is in place irrespective of whether the partnership's principal place of business is outside the United States or all its members are foreign persons. A foreign partnership required to file a return must report all of its foreign and U.S. source income. A foreign partnership with U.S. source income is not required to file a federal annual return if it qualifies for a *de minimis* exception (generally, the partnership had no effectively connected income during its tax year, had U.S. source income of USD 20 000 or less during its tax year, and less than 1% of any partnership item of income, gain, loss, deduction or credit is allocated in the aggregate to direct U.S. partners, or foreign partnerships with no U.S. partners and no effectively connected income).

Ownership information held by the partnership or partners

98.   Pursuant to I.R.C. section 6001, every taxpayer or filer of an annual return, including partnerships, must keep books and records sufficient to establish amounts reported in a return. These books and records include the books and records required to satisfy the reporting requirements described above, including ownership reporting on Forms 1065 and 8858 and Schedules K-1 and, in the case of owners that are not U.S. persons, reporting and withholding certificates with respect to effectively connected taxable income and all fixed, determinable, annual, or periodical gains, profit, or income.

99.   In order to meet the various tax reporting requirements with respect to ownership information, as described, partnerships must hold the requisite information. In addition, the ULPA section 111(a) and DLPA section 17-305(a) (3) require that the partnership have available upon the request of any limited partner the full name and address of each partner. Similarly, the DLCCA in section 18-305(a)(3) requires that an LLC have and make available to any member upon request, a current list of all members and managers and their addresses. See DLLCA § 305(a)(3). See also ULLCA § 410.

100.   Equivalent or stronger record keeping requirements are found in the California, Florida, New York and Texas Limited Liability Company Acts. For example, the New York Limited Liability Company Law (2006) contains specific record keeping requirements in Section 1102 which provide that the LLC must keep a "current list of the full name set forth in alphabetical order and the last known mailing address of each member together with the contribution and the share of profits and losses of each member or information from which such share can be readily derived." Similarly, the Florida Limited Liability Company Act (1999) provides that an LLC must keep a "current list of the full names and last known business, residence, or mailing addresses of all members and managers" and, unless it is contained in the Articles of Organization, "the amount of cash and a description and statement of the agreed value of any other property or services contributed by each member and which each member has agreed to contribute" (Sec. 608.4101). The corresponding requirement in California Limited Liability Company Act is to keep a list of the full name and last known business or residence address of each member and of each holder of an economic interest in the LLC, along with the contribution and the share in profits and losses of each (Sec. 17058).

101.   Information concerning the identity of partners in partnerships is available in any case where the partnership is subject to tax filing requirements. This will be the case for all partnerships formed under U.S. law or that carry on business or have income, deductions or credits for U.S. federal income tax purposes. Furthermore, this includes LLCs that are taxed as partnerships for federal income tax purposes. Where a LLC has only one member, however, it will not be treated as a partnership and tax filing obligations may not apply.

Single Member LLCs

102.   A domestic entity organized as an LLC with a single member is not classified as a partnership for tax purposes (since a partnership requires at least two members) and will be disregarded as an entity separate from its owner for U.S. federal income tax purposes if it does not elect corporate tax treatment. This means that, for tax purposes, the assets and liabilities of the LLC are treated as assets and liabilities of the LLC's owner. Not being a separate

entity for tax purposes, such an entity does not file a separate annual return. The owner of the LLC is treated as owning directly all the assets of the LLC. Whether the owner has any U.S. federal tax filing requirements will depend on the owner's status (*e.g.* as a resident or non-resident) and the nature of the income generated by the assets held through the LLC (*e.g.* U.S. source or non-U.S. source) and the activities of the LLC. A U.S. citizen or resident would report the income in the same manner as it would with any asset that the person owned directly. A foreign owner of a disregarded LLC would only have U.S. federal tax obligations as a result of its ownership of the LLC if the LLC were engaged in a U.S. trade or business or if the assets were otherwise generating U.S. source income. This will often be the case, as LLCs are widely used for structuring investments into the United States and for many other legitimate business reasons.[5] Where, however, the single-member LLC is not engaged in a U.S. trade or business, has no fixed, determinable, annual, or periodical gains, profits, or income, and does not otherwise have a tax nexus with the United States, there is no obligation to file a federal income tax return with the IRS.

103.   The United States relies to a large extent on tax filing obligations to ensure the availability of ownership information in the case of LLCs. Where a single member LLC has no tax filing obligations reliance must then be placed on state law to ensure that this information is available.

104.   Pursuant to State laws, an LLC must know who its members are (see above) but ownership information is generally not required to be provided to the State's authorities, either at the time the LLC is formed or subsequently. Neither is it required to be kept in the United States. Similarly, only limited information may be required to be reported in respect of the LLC's management. All states require that a registered agent be appointed for service of process. This agent is not required to know the owners of the company. Accordingly, where a single member LLC has no tax nexus with the United States there may be no information available in the United States regarding the owners of that LLC.[6]

105.   Delaware law requires that a "communications contact" be provided:

> (g) *Every limited liability company formed under the laws of the State of Delaware or qualified to do business in the State of*

---

5.   LLCs are widely used in cross border business transactions because of their relatively low costs and hybrid nature.

6.   Essential to the formation of an LLC is that an agreement between the members must exist that governs the relations between them. There is no general requirement that the agreement be in writing, though typically this will be the case where there is more than one member. In the context of a single-member LLC, an agreement is still required. Operating agreements do not have to be filed with any governmental authority.

> *Delaware shall provide to its registered agent and update from time to time as necessary the name, business address and business telephone number of a natural person who is a member, manager, officer, employee or designated agent of the limited liability company, who is then authorized to receive communications from the registered agent. Such person shall be deemed the communications contact for the limited liability company. Every registered agent shall retain (in paper or electronic form) the above information concerning the current communications contact for each limited liability company and each foreign limited liability company for which that registered agent serves as registered agent. If the limited liability company fails to provide the registered agent with a current communications contact, the registered agent may resign as the registered agent for such limited liability company pursuant to this section. (DLLCA § 18-104(g))*

106. While the communications contact provides the identity of a natural person, this person is merely authorised to receive communications on behalf of the LLC from the registered agent, and there is no necessity for that person to have ownership information regarding the LLC. Where that person is outside the territorial jurisdiction of the United States, there is no guarantee that they would receive or respond to any communication from the IRS. Moreover, the only consequence for failure to provide the identity of the communications contact to the registered agent is that the registered agent may resign on that basis.

107. The FATF have rated the United States non-compliant in relation to its Recommendation 33 (Legal Persons – Beneficial Ownership). Peer jurisdictions have also identified issues relating to obtaining ownership information regarding Delaware entities or LLCs in general. Some raised concerns about the legal framework for ensuring the availability of this information, and in other cases peers cited examples where requests for information were unanswered. The IRS can, and does, use its information-gathering powers to inquire into ownership information in these cases, but the effectiveness of these powers will be limited where the information is not held by any person within the United States' territorial jurisdiction.

108. It should also be noted that in practice, requests for information relating to LLCs is small compared with the EOI program in general. The IRS considers that these requests comprise only a small percentage of cases, and this is consistent with the peer input received. The IRS considers that it successfully responds to a large subset of such requests.

109. The United States has been working to address concerns raised by the FATF, but the process is lengthy given the difficulties of coordinating changes at state level (see Mutual Evaluation Follow-up Reports in 2008,

2009 and 2010). Recently, however, it has taken a number of affirmative steps to curb the opportunities for abuse by single member LLCs exploiting the inaccessibility of ownership information (see *Recent Developments*, above).

Trusts (ToR A.1.4)

110.   In the United States, trusts generally are created either by a Last Will and Testament on death, or by a written declaration or trust agreement executed by the settlor during life. In each case, the trustee takes legal title to property for the purpose of protecting, managing and/or conserving it for the benefit of the trust beneficiaries, the equitable title holders, in accordance with the terms of the trust and applicable state law. The creation, funding, and administration of trusts are matters of state (and not federal) law. Information concerning trustees, settlors and beneficiaries of trusts that are subject to state law or federal income tax law is available. Trusts that are treated as foreign trusts for U.S. federal income tax purposes, but that have a U.S. resident trustee may often be subject to state law requirements to know the settlors, trustees and beneficiaries of a trust, whether or not the trust is governed by foreign law. There may be limited circumstances where a trustee resident in the United States, acting as the trustee of a foreign trust, is not subject to any U.S. rules regarding the maintenance of such information. There is, however, a strong likelihood that the trustee would in any event know the identity of the settlors and beneficiaries, and the trustee would be subject to the jurisdiction of a U.S. court and the IRS summons power. As a practical matter, the availability of information on trusts has not posed any problems for exchange of information purposes.

Trust ownership and identity information held by the Trust

111.   In order to fulfil their fiduciary duties in respect of trusts governed by U.S. law, a trustee must generally know the identity of any other trustee, of the settlor(s) and the identity of all beneficiaries. If family relationship is relevant (for example, for distributions to be made *per stirpes*), it will also be important for the trustee to know the lineage of each beneficiary (*i.e.* the beneficiary's place on the family tree). In the case of a discretionary trust, the trustee has a fiduciary obligation to know who is included in the class of permissible beneficiaries of the trust, in order to properly exercise the trustee's discretion regarding whether or not to make distributions to one or more such beneficiaries. To the extent a trustee does not maintain this information, the trustee may become liable for damages for a breach of the trustee's fiduciary obligations if, for example, the lack of information hinders the trustee's ability to make appropriate decisions and/or provide required communications to beneficiaries. (See Restatement Third, Trusts § 32.)

112.   Inherent in a trustee's obligations as trustee is his or her duty of loyalty to the beneficiaries, which can only be discharged if the beneficiaries are

known to the trustee (Restatement Third, Trusts, s. 78, Uniform Trust Code, s. 802). In addition, a trustee has an obligation to maintain adequate records, which is implicit in the duty to act with prudence (Uniform Trust Code, s. 804) and the duty to report to beneficiaries (Uniform Trust Code, s. 813).

Trust ownership and identity information required to be provided to government authorities

113.   The United States classifies trusts for purposes of U.S. federal taxation as either domestic trusts or foreign trusts. A trust is treated as a domestic trust if: (1) a court within the United States is able to exercise primary supervision over the administration of the trust (court test); and (2) one or more U.S. persons have the authority to control all substantial trust decisions (control test). I.R.C. § 7701(a)(30)(E). Treas. Reg. §301.7701-7. A foreign trust is any trust that fails to meet the statutory definition of a domestic trust. I.R.C. § 7701(a)(31)(B). In practice, a trust formed under the laws of a U.S. state will generally be a domestic trust, so long as it meets the court and control tests, and a trust formed under the laws of a foreign jurisdiction will generally be a foreign trust.

114.   All domestic trusts (with a few limited exceptions, such as a grantor trust using the grantor's Social Security number as its taxpayer identification number), and all foreign trusts that earn income that is effectively connected with a U.S. trade or business, or that otherwise are required to file a U.S. return, are required to obtain an employer identification number (EIN) by filing an application with the IRS that identifies the trust and trustee and the address of each. This EIN must be provided to each bank, broker, or other entity when opening an account or purchasing property in the name of the trust. A charitable trust will be issued an EIN when it files an application for recognition of tax exempt status, a return that will contain the name and address of the trust and the trustee as well as additional information regarding the trust's sources of support, intended activities, and anticipated budget for three years.

115.   A trustee of a domestic trust generally has both state and federal tax filing obligations as a fiduciary of the trust. The trustee and/or U.S. beneficiary and/or U.S. owner of a foreign trust also will have federal tax filing obligations in certain circumstances.

116.   In the case of a taxable domestic trust, the trustee(s) must file Form 1041, U.S. Income Tax Return for Estates and Trusts, with the IRS for each year in which the trust has (see Treas. Reg. § 1.6012-3(a)(1)):

- Any taxable income for the taxable year,

- Gross income of USD 600 or more (regardless of taxable income), or

- A beneficiary who is a non-resident alien.

117.   Form 1041 requires that any trustee (fiduciary) of the trust be iden-tified and that each beneficiary of the trust who received trust income in that year be identified on a separate schedule. The identifying information provided in respect of the beneficiary includes their identifying number (*e.g.* Social Security Number), name and address.

118.   It is essential that each trustee maintain records regarding the name of the settlor given that the special tax rules will apply depending on the identity of the settlor (see discussion of grantor trusts below). If the genera-tion-skipping transfer tax may apply to the trust and not all beneficiaries are family members of the settlor, the trustee must also know the date of birth of the settlor. With regard to certain charitable and other tax exempt or split-interest trusts, the trustee may also be required to know the settlor's address, and the nature of the settlor's relationships, if any, with other individuals or entities so that the trust may be administered without violating any of the applicable rules regarding self-dealing and other such issues.

119.   Certain special rules apply in the case of a grantor trust. In general, a trust is a grantor trust if either the settlor or some other person holds certain powers over the trust or the right to certain economic benefits from the trust assets. Certain foreign trusts created by a U.S. person with U.S. beneficiar-ies will be treated as grantor trusts (see I.R.C. § 679). In general, that person is treated as the owner of the trust's assets for federal income tax purposes. As a result, all of the income, deductions, and credits of the grantor trust are treated as belonging to the deemed owner of the trust, and are reported on that owner's personal income tax return. I.R.C. § 671 and Rev. Rul. 85-13. A grantor trust must file Form 1041 unless the trust is eligible to file under one of the optional filing methods. See Treas. Reg. § 1.671-4(b). Under the optional methods, a Form 1041 need not be filed but other reporting require-ments apply. A grantor trust that is a foreign trust, a trust with assets located outside of the United States, and a trust owned wholly or in part by a foreign person generally will be required to file a Form 1040-NR and will not be eligible for the optional filing methods of Treas. Reg § 1.671-4(b). See Treas Reg. § 1.671-4(b)(6). In the case of a foreign trust where a U.S. person is considered to own the trust assets under the grantor trust rules (I.R.C. § 671-679), each U.S. person treated as an owner of a foreign trust is responsible for ensuring that the foreign trust annually files a Form 3520-A, setting forth a full and complete accounting of all trust activities, trust operations and other relevant information concerning the trust.

Trust ownership and identity information held by service providers

120.   Under the Bank Secrecy Act regulations, a trust company organ-ized under the laws of any state or of the United States is included in the definition of a bank (31 C.F.R. § 103.11(c)(1)) and of a financial institution

(31 C.F.R. § 103.11(n)(1)). Accordingly, the customer identification requirements of 31 C.F.R. § 103.121 are applicable to trust companies providing "trust services" (whether or not in the capacity of a trustee), and require that the trust company identify its customer by obtaining information including the customer's name, date of birth, address (for an individual), and Taxpayer Identification Number (or other government issued documentation identifying the customer in the case of a non-U.S. person).

Foreign Trusts

121.   Trusts that are treated as a foreign trust for income tax purposes where the trustee is resident in the United States, may not have any tax reporting obligations if there is no U.S. owner of the trust and no other nexus with the U.S. Where the trust is governed by state law, the rules discussed above regarding the fiduciary obligations of the trustee would generally apply. If the trust is formed pursuant to foreign law, U.S. law provides that the administration and management of the trust, including the respective duties and obligations of the trustee and beneficiaries, may nevertheless be governed by the law of a different jurisdiction – specifically, the U.S. state in which the trust is administered. (See Restatement (Second) of Conflict of Laws §271 and Comments; *Wilmington Trust Co. v. Wilmington Trust Co.,* 21 Del. Ch. 188, 186 A. 903 (1936); *Russell v. Lovell,* 362 Mass. 794, 291 N.E.2d 733 (1973); and *Brown v. Ryan,* 338 Ill. App. 3d 864, 273 Ill. Dec. 307, 788 N.E.2d 1183 (1st Dist. 2003).). The jurisdiction where the trust is administered may be determined based on a variety of factors, each of which may be given different weight depending upon the facts of the particular case, but the location of the trustee and where the trustee actively performs the trustee's duties will carry significant weight. Therefore, where a foreign trust is considered to be administered in a U.S. state by virtue of the fact that the trustee is resident in that state, then the trustee may be subject to that state's trust law relating to the trust's administration. Where this is the case, information concerning settlors, trustees and beneficiaries will be available. In addition, all U.S. trustees with signatory authority over the foreign financial account of any trust, including a trust formed pursuant to foreign trust law, are required to file an FBAR with regard to the accounts of such trusts, in addition to any other applicable filing obligation.

122.   In summary, trusts formed under foreign law may be considered domestic trusts for U.S. federal income tax purposes or the trustee may be subject to anti-money laundering customer due diligence rules or the state law may apply to the trustee in respect of the administration of the trust. In these cases, there are laws in place that require information concerning trustees, settlors and beneficiaries to be maintained. Where these circumstances cited do not apply, a trustee resident in the United States may not be subject

to any U.S. rules regarding the maintenance of such information. There is, however, a strong likelihood that the trustee would in any event know the identity of the settlors and beneficiaries, and the trustee would be subject to the jurisdiction of a U.S. court and the IRS summons power. As a practical matter, the availability of information on trusts has not posed any problems for exchange of information purposes. It is also conceivable that a trust could be created which has no connection with the United States other than that the settlor chooses that the trust will be governed by the laws of one of the states. In that event there may be no information about the trust available in the United States.

Foundations (ToR A.1.5)

123. It is not possible to form a foundation in the United States as a distinct legal entity. Organisations may be referred to as "foundations", however, these are formed as companies or trusts.

Enforcement provisions to ensure availability of information (ToR A.1.6)

124. The IRS vigorously enforces the Internal Revenue Code, as evidenced by the fact that some USD 36 billion in civil penalties were assessed in 2009, including over USD 445 million in penalties related to non-filing. The IRS also initiated 4 121 criminal investigations in 2009.

125. There are substantial civil and criminal penalties under federal tax law for noncompliance with the tax filing and information reporting requirements. Failure to file a return (including Form 1120) incurs a penalty up to 25% of the tax owed. I.R.C. §6651. Where a false corporate tax return is filed wilfully, criminal penalties of up to USD 500 000 and 3 years of imprisonment may be imposed. I.R.C. § 7206. In cases of negligence or substantial understatement of tax there is an addition to tax of 20%. I.R.C. §6662. In cases of civil fraud, the addition is 75%. I.R.C. §6663. Additionally, in the case of a failure to file a complete Form 5472, a civil penalty attaches in the amount of USD 10 000 per related party, and if the failure continues more than 90 days after notice by the IRS, USD 10 000 for each 30-day period that the failure continues. I.R.C. § 6038A(d). A wide variety of other penalties apply for other filing requirements, including failure to file information returns.

126. In general, if a withholding agent fails to obtain a Form W-8 from a foreign person, the withholding agent must withhold 30% of any amount that is subject to withholding and paid to that foreign person. Every withholding agent who withholds tax is required to deposit such tax with an authorized financial institution. A withholding agent must make an income tax return for

income paid during the preceding calendar year. Penalties for failure to make deposits of tax (IRC Sec. 6656) vary and may be up to 10% of the underpayment if the failure is more than 15 days. Where a person fails to collect and pay over tax (IRC Sec. 6672) they may be liable to a penalty equal to the total amount of the tax evaded, or not collected, or not accounted for and paid over. Where this failure is wilful the person is guilty of a felony and, liable to a fine of up to USD 10 000, or imprisonment for up to 5 years, or both.

127.   Should a corporation, limited partnership, or LLC fail to maintain the ownership information required under the applicable state law, an owner of the entity can bring an action against the entity for failing to maintain the information, which could result in a judgment requiring the disclosure and in some cases a monetary damage award.

128.   On the criminal side, any person required to pay any tax, or required to make a return (including information returns), keep any records, or supply any information, who wilfully fails to pay such tax, make such return, keep such records, or supply such information, at the time or times required by law or regulations, shall, in addition to other penalties provided by law, be guilty of a misdemeanor and, upon conviction thereof, be fined not more than USD 25 000 (USD 100 000 in the case of a corporation) or imprisoned not more than 1 year, or both, together with the costs of prosecution. I.R.C. § 7203. Where a false corporate tax return is filed wilfully, criminal penalties of up to USD 500 000 and 3 years of imprisonment may be imposed. I.R.C. § 7206.

129.   A partnership's failure to file an annual return (Form 1065) subjects it to a penalty based on the number of partners the partnership has and the number of months late the return is filed, subject to a cap. I.R.C. § 6698. To the extent that the failure to file a partnership return results in partners' failure to report income from the partnership appropriately, the range of substantial civil and criminal penalties under federal tax law for noncompliance with the partners' own tax filing requirements could apply. For example, a partner's failure to file a return incurs a penalty up to 25% of the tax owed. I.R.C. § 6651. In cases of negligence or substantial understatement of tax there is an addition to tax of 20%. I.R.C. § 6662. In cases of civil fraud, the addition is 75%. I.R.C. § 6663. Where a false partnership return is filed wilfully, criminal penalties of up to USD 500 000 and 3 years of imprisonment may be imposed. I.R.C. § 7206.

130. In respect of trusts, there are potentially significant civil penalties under State law that may be imposed on a trustee who breaches the trustee's fiduciary obligations to the trust beneficiaries and/or accounting obligations to a beneficiary and/or US court.

131.   Wilful failure to file an information return is addressed by I.R.C. section 7203, which provides that any person required to pay any tax, or required to make a return (including information returns), keep any records, or supply any information, who wilfully fails to pay such tax, make such return, keep such records, or supply such information, at the time or times required by law or regulations, shall, in addition to other penalties provided by law, be guilty of a misdemeanor and, upon conviction thereof, be fined not more than USD 25 000 (USD 100 000 in the case of a corporation) or imprisoned not more than 1 year, or both, together with the costs of prosecution.

132.   When a person presumed to be in possession or control of the information refuses to comply with a request, the IRS will serve a summons on that person. This will include any person subject to the jurisdiction of the U.S. courts, including the trustee of a foreign trust. The IRS has broad powers to issue a summons to a taxpayer or third-party for information (including witness testimony under oath) and documents. The IRS summons will be directed to the taxpayer or a third-party, including an officer or employee of a taxpayer, with possession, custody, or care of relevant and material evidence. See I.R.C. § 7602. The administrative summons power under I.R.C. section 7602 *et seq.* is limited only to information that exists. If the information is not required to be kept, but the record exists, the record may be summoned. The summons powers also include the ability to depose persons on requests made under a relevant tax treaty. Thus, the U.S. Competent Authority has plenary authority to obtain ownership, identity and accounting information from persons not required to have such information, but that are in possession of, or have control of and are able to obtain, such information.

133.   The penalties for failing to comply with a summons apply regardless of whether the person is required to have the information. If the summonsed party is in possession, custody, or control of information or documents, that person must comply or assert why he/she cannot or will not comply. In general, the only exceptions to compliance are certain privileges generally recognized by exchange-of-information treaties and TIEAs (*i.e.* attorney-client privilege; trade, business, industrial, commercial, or professional secrets; and information the disclosure of which would be contrary to public policy). Consequences for failure to comply with a summons for non-privileged information or documents can be harsh and, therefore, are a strong deterrent for noncompliance. If any person fails to comply with a summons, the U.S. district court for the district in which that person resides or is found has jurisdiction to compel compliance. See I.R.C. § 7604. The U.S. district court may hold the noncompliant person in contempt of court, which may entail fines and/or imprisonment, in order to compel compliance. Additionally, a person may be prosecuted for noncompliance and subject to monetary penalties and/or imprisonment of up to one year. See I.R.C. § 7210.

Determination and factors underlying recommendations

Phase 1 Determination	
The element is in place, but certain aspects of the legal implementation of the element need improvement.	
Factors underlying recommendations	**Recommendations**
Ownership and identity information for single member LLCs is not always available.	The United States should take all necessary steps to ensure that information concerning the owners of all LLCs is available.

Phase 2 Rating
To be finalised as soon as a representative subset of Phase 2 reviews is completed

A.2. Accounting records

> Jurisdictions should ensure that reliable accounting records are kept for all relevant entities and arrangements.

General requirements (ToR A.2.1)

134.   The requirement to maintain adequate accounting records is generally satisfied by the application of federal tax law to companies, trusts and partnerships. However, other federal law and state law provisions are also relevant.

Federal Law

135.   Under the IRC's general record maintenance requirement (I.R.C. §6001), any person subject to income tax, or any person required to file a return of information with respect to income, is required to keep such permanent books of account or records, including inventories, as are necessary to establish the amount of gross income, deductions, credits, or other matters required to be shown by such person in any return of such tax or information. Treas. Reg. § 1.6001-1(a). The required accounting records include the taxpayer's regular books of account and such other records and data as may be necessary to support the entries on the taxpayer's books of account and on the taxpayer's return, for example, a reconciliation of any differences between such books and the return. See Treas. Reg. § 1.446-1.

136.   Corporations and partnerships generally must provide as a schedule to their annual return a balance sheet that agrees with their books and records, as well as a schedule that reconciles their income or loss per their books of account

with income per their annual return. For a corporation the schedule generally reconciles financial statement net income (loss) for the corporation (or consolidated financial statement group, if applicable) to the corporation's net income (loss) for U.S. taxable income purposes (IRS Form 1120 Schedules L, M-1, and M-3). For a partnership, the schedule similarly generally reconciles income per the accounting income statement of the partnership with income (loss) per the return (IRS Form 1065, Schedules L, M-1, and M-3). The records required under I.R.C. §§ 6038A and 6038C for "reporting corporations" include all information, documents or other records relevant to determining the correct U.S. tax treatment of transactions with foreign related parties. To be deemed sufficient, such records must include, to the extent relevant to the taxpayer's business, (i) original entry books and transaction records; (ii) cost data from which the reporting corporation can compile and supply within a reasonable time, material profit and loss statements with respect to U.S.-connected products or services; (iii) pricing documents; (iv) financial documents filed with financial institutions or foreign governments; (v) ownership and capital structure records; (vi) records of loans, services and other non-sales transactions; (vii) and records relating to conduit financing arrangements. Treas. Reg. § 1.6038A-3(c)(2).

137.   Federal Securities Law (Section 13(b)(2) of the Securities Exchange Act) requires the preparation and maintenance of books and records in "reasonable detail" that "accurately and fairly reflect" the transactions and dispositions of assets. This requirement (*i.e.* application of generally accepted accounting principles) applies to all companies that have securities registered under that Act as well as on all companies required to file reports pursuant to the Exchange Act – that is, public or reporting companies.

State Law – companies

138.   In addition to the federal law requirements, both the MBCA and Delaware law require corporations to keep adequate books and records, including accounting records. MBCA § 16.01 (b), see also; DGCL § 220. "Appropriate" records for the purposes of the MBCA are generally records that permit financial statements to be prepared which fairly present the financial position and transactions of the corporation. In some very small businesses operating on a cash basis, "appropriate" accounting records may consist only of a check register, vouchers, and receipts.

139.   Similar requirements apply under the California Corporations Code, the Florida Business Corporations Act, the New York Business Corporation Law, the Pennsylvania Associations Code and the Texas Business Organizations Code.[7] While there may be no specific penalty for failing to keep accounting

---

7.   For example, pursuant to section 607.1601 (Corporate Records) of the Florida Business Corporations Act a corporation must maintain "accurate accounting

records these statutes typically provide that a Court can compel the production of accounting information or order that a corporation to make it available to shareholders.

140.   It may be noted that, under U.S. corporate law generally, record maintenance also helps preserve the limited liability of a corporation's owners. Limited liability may be pierced, with the result that a parent corporation or a controlling individual shareholder may be held liable for the acts of a controlled corporation, under circumstances that vary depending on the cause of action and other factors. A key factor in a successful defence showing that corporate separation should be respected is scrupulous maintenance of separate books and observance of corporate formalities. See, *e.g.* United States v. Fidelity Capital Corp., 920 F.2d 827 (11th Cir. Ga. 1991) and Briggs Transp. Co. v. Starr Sales Co., 262 N.W.2d 805, 810 (Iowa 1978).

141.   A wide variety of state and local law provisions outside state corporate law (for instance, state and local income tax and state and local sales tax law) also require detailed accounting records to be kept. Most states have general rules as well as additional rules that are specific to industries or categories of companies. The specifics of these rules will vary by state or locality.

State Law – partnerships

142.   In addition to the federal law requirements to keep accounting records imposed as a result of the obligation to file U.S. federal annual returns, under state law, partners of a partnership generally may bring an action for an accounting and may have a cause of action against other partners or managers for failure to maintain records adequate to determine the partners' relative interests. In addition, the ULPA (§ 111) requires that numerous records, including three years of financial statements, must be maintained at its designated office, and the DLPA §17-305(a) requires that the partnership make available to any limited partner true and full information regarding the status of the business and financial condition of the limited partnership, including a record of the partners' contributions and copies of the partnership's annual returns. Limited partnerships also must maintain records adequate to support distributions. DLPA §17-607.

143.   For limited liability companies, although there is generally no specific requirement to maintain *adequate* accounting records, state laws generally require that LLCs maintain financial and other relevant information.

---

records". A corporation must also provide financial statements to shareholders. Similarly, Section 1500 of the California Corporations requires that "Each corporation shall keep adequate and correct books and records of account."

In some states, including Texas, California, and Florida,[8] these are direct requirements. More frequently states impose this requirement indirectly. For example, Delaware law requires that an LLC provide to each member upon request true and full information regarding the status of the business and financial condition of the LLC, as well as a record of members' contributions and copies of tax returns (DLLCA §18-305(a)). The Uniform LLC Act contains a similar requirement (ULLCA §410). In addition, LLCs have to maintain records adequate to support distributions to members (DLLCA § 18-607; ULLCA § 405).

144.   Delaware law does not specify what "information regarding the status of the business and financial condition" of the company consists of, nor the

---

8.   There are requirements to keep accounting records. For example in Florida rules against impairment of capital provide (Florida LLC Act, Section 608.426):

(1) The limited liability company may make distributions to its members in accordance with the provisions contained in the operating agreement, except that no distribution may be made if after the distribution the limited liability company would be insolvent. If the operating agreement does not provide for the payment of distributions to members, the distributions shall be made on the basis of the agreed value, as stated in the records of the limited liability company, of the contributions made by each member to the extent they have been received by the limited liability company and have not been returned.

(2) The managers or managing members of a limited liability company may base a determination that a distribution is not prohibited under subsection (1) either on financial statements prepared on the basis of accounting practices and principles that are reasonable in the circumstances or on a fair valuation or other method that is reasonable in the circumstances. In the case of any distribution based upon such financial statement or such a valuation, each such distribution shall be identified as a distribution based upon such financial statements or a fair valuation of assets, and the amount distributed shall be disclosed to the receiving members concurrent with their receipt of the distribution.

Other provisions of the Florida LLC Act require copies of the limited liability company's federal, state, and local income tax returns and reports, if any, for the 3 most recent years, and, copies of any then-effective operating agreement and any financial statements of the limited liability company for the 3 most recent years to be maintained.

The LLC must also maintain a writing setting out: (1). The amount of cash and a description and statement of the agreed value of any other property or services contributed by each member and which each member has agreed to contribute, and (2). The times at which or events on the happening of which any additional contributions agreed to be made by each member are to be made.

types of records needed to support distributions. For LLCs that are taxed as corporations or partnerships (and so subject to tax filing and record-keeping obligations), this absence of a specific requirement to maintain accounting records is less significant. For a single-member LLC that has no federal tax reporting obligations, there may be no other requirements placed on it, and any obligation to provide information to its owner or to support a distribution may not have significant weight as there may not be any penalty or adverse consequence where they are dispensed with.

145.   There are a wide variety of state and local law provisions outside state corporate law (for instance, state and local income tax and state and local sales tax law) that may also require accounting records to be kept. However, gaps may occur where there is no state-level taxation and where the entity is not carrying on a trade or business in any of the states.

State Law – Trusts

146.   In order to properly administer the trust in accordance with state law and the trustee's fiduciary obligations, the trustee must maintain adequate books and records. Section 83 of the Restatement of Trust law, 3rd, states:

> *Implicit in the duty to provide information to beneficiaries (§ 82) is the duty stated in this Section requiring a trustee to maintain an adequate set of books and records. The performance of these record-keeping responsibilities is also essential to a trustee's duty to collect and safeguard the trust property (§ 76, Comment d) and to the beneficiaries' right to enforce the trustee's duty to act with prudence, loyalty, and impartiality (§§ 77-79), as well as the trustee's duty regarding reasonable and appropriate costs of administration (§ 88). Accordingly, the trustee has a duty to maintain books (or accounts) and records that show in detail the nature and amount of the trust property and the trustee's administration thereof.*

147.   The same requirement is contained in section 810 of the Uniform Trust Code. It is also a fundamental duty of the trustee to keep the beneficiaries reasonably informed of the administration of the trust (Uniform Trust Code, s. 813). As noted above (see section A1.4), even where a trust is created pursuant to foreign law, the administration of the trust may be governed by the law of the state in which the trust is administered, which is often considered to be the state where the trustee is resident. Consequently, state law regarding the duty to maintain accounting records may in some cases apply to foreign law trusts having a U.S. resident trustee. Furthermore, the trust may be considered a domestic trust for federal income tax purposes or the trustee may be subject to anti-money laundering due diligence rules and therefore be required to maintain accounting information. There may

be limited circumstances where a trustee resident in the United States is not subject to any U.S. rules regarding the maintenance of such information and any requirement to maintain accounting information may depend on foreign law. As a practical matter, the availability of information on trusts has not posed any problems for exchange of information purposes. It is also the case that, in these circumstances, the trustee would be subject to the jurisdiction of a U.S. court and the IRS summons power.

Underlying documentation (ToR A.2.2)

148.   The required accounting records to be kept by taxpayers under the tax law include the taxpayer's regular books of account and such other records and data as may be necessary to support the entries on the taxpayer's books of account and on the taxpayer's return, for example, a reconciliation of any differences between such books and the return. See Treas. Reg. § 1.446-1. This requirement will cover companies, partnerships and trusts that are subject to U.S. federal income tax reporting. However, LLCs that are disregarded for federal income tax purposes and have no tax nexus to the United States, and trusts that are treated as foreign trusts for federal income tax purposes will not be subject to these rules. As discussed above, the laws governing LLCs do not generally impose a requirement to maintain adequate accounting records and consequently there may not be a requirement to maintain any underlying documentation either.

149.   In the case of any trust formed pursuant to U.S. law (regardless of whether the trust is treated as a foreign trust for federal income tax purposes), trustees generally have a duty to be prepared to account to trust beneficiaries and/or the local court under state law and/or the trust instrument (as described in § 813 of the Uniform Trust Code). Such an account consists of a detailed listing of every dollar received and every dollar disbursed by the trust during the period covered by that account, along with a listing of all of the assets of the trust held at the end of that accounting period. The preparation of such an account requires the retention of the records necessary to identify and support the purpose and exact amount of each receipt and disbursement, as well as account statements verifying both the transactions during the accounting period and the balance held at the end of that period. In addition, under federal tax law, books and records required to support information on a federal tax or information return must be retained for as long as the contents thereof may become material in the administration of any internal revenue law. Treas. Reg. under § 6001. This requirement applies to trustees of trusts.

150.   As noted above (see section A1.4), even where a trust is created pursuant to foreign law, the administration of the trust may be governed by the law of the state in which the trust is administered, which is often considered

to be the state where the trustee is resident. Consequently, state law regarding the duty to maintain accounting records will in many cases apply to foreign law trusts having a U.S. resident trustee. There may be limited circumstances where a trustee resident in the United States acting as the trustee of a foreign trust is not subject to any U.S. rules regarding the maintenance of such information, and any requirement to maintain accounting information may depend on foreign law. To date this has not impeded effective exchange of information. It is also the case that the trustee in these circumstances would be subject to the jurisdiction of a U.S. court and the IRS summons power, as well as the requirement to file an FBAR.

5-year retention standard (ToR A.2.3)

151.   For federal income tax purposes, the basic rule is that taxpayers are required to retain the required applicable books or records so long as the contents thereof may become material in tax administration, which normally is at least as long as the period of limitations for assessment of tax remains open. See Treas. Reg. §§ 1.6001-1(e), 1.6038A-3(g). The generally applicable period of limitations for assessment is three years from the date the return is due, or if the return is filed after the due date, three years from the date the return is actually filed. I.R.C. § 6501(a). However, where a specified information reporting requirement applies, including that under I.R.C. section 6038A with respect to 25%-foreign-owned U.S. corporations, the limitations period does not expire earlier than three years following production of the required information. I.R.C. § 6501(c)(8).

152.   In addition, if there is a substantial omission from gross income on the return, the period of limitations for assessment is six years. I.R.C. § 6501(e). In the case of a fraudulent or false return or the failure to file a return, the period of limitations remains open indefinitely. I.R.C. § 6501(c)(1).

153.   Tax returns are always due at some point after the tax year has closed, so the period of limitations for assessment is always greater than three years from the end of the tax year. As noted, in many instances, the period of limitations for assessment is greater and may be indefinite. In particular, because the assertion of a substantial omission from gross income by the IRS may trigger a six-year period of limitations, taxpayers have strong incentives to retain records for at least six years. In the case of an individual taxpayer whose only income is a salary, it may be possible to dispose of the tax receipt in respect of his salary and pay slips for the year 3 years following the filing of his or her tax return for that year. Conversely, the greater the complexity of the taxpayers' affairs, the more likely that records will have to be maintained for a longer period, either to rebut the assertion that there has been a substantial omission or because the records continue to relate to items that are relevant for the assessment of tax. A leading reference on federal

corporate taxation notes that for purposes of determining earnings and profits of a U.S. corporation for tax purposes, "it may be necessary to decide how a transaction occurring many years ago should have been treated under a long-interred statute because of its effect on accumulated earnings and profits; and, because there is no statute of limitations governing the effect of prior transactions on accumulated earnings and profits, it is advisable to retain corporate records permanently."[9]

State Law

154.   Both DLPA §17-607(b) and the DLLCA §18-607(b) provide that a limited partner or member is liable to the limited partnership or LLC (for up to a three year period) to return a distribution that it received with knowledge that such distribution was improperly made in violation of the statute. This provides a strong incentive for partners or members to ensure that a limited partnership or LLC retains records for at least three years following any distribution, and effectively functions as an implicit record retention require-ment. In other words, a partner or member will want the limited partnership or LLC to retain adequate books and records relating to the assets of the entity for at least three years following a distribution in the event that it need to prove that such distribution was properly made in compliance with the requirements of the statute for making a distribution. For example, in the event that a creditor asserted a claim against a limited partnership or LLC within the three year period following the making of a distribution, and the limited partnership or LLC had improperly made a distribution to a limited partner or member of which such person had knowledge, such limited partner or member may have to return such distribution to the limited partnership or LLC to enable the entity to satisfy the liability to the creditor. It would therefore be important in that instance that the limited partnership or LLC have adequate books and records to prove that the distribution itself was not improper at the time it was made and as a result not subject to return by the limited partner or member (setting aside whether or not, if the distribution was in fact improper, they would have had knowledge of it).

155.   In order to properly administer a trust in accordance with state law and the trustee's fiduciary obligations, the trustee generally may be required to retain information regarding the settlor, trustee and beneficiaries for at least several years after the death of each such person and for several years after the termination of the trust, and is likely to be required to retain such information indefinitely. Section 1005 of the Uniform Trust Code provides that, in the absence of adequate disclosure of certain actions of the trustee, an action for breach of fiduciary duty may be commenced within five years after

---

9.   Bittker & Eustice, Federal Taxation of Corporations and Shareholders, at 8.03.

the first of the following to occur: the removal, resignation, or death of the trustee; the termination of the beneficiary's interest in the trust; or the termination of the trust. Section 107 of ERISA requires the sponsor of a qualified plan and trust to retain worksheets and other supporting records related to the Form 5500 for at least six years after the date of the filing. In addition, section 209 of ERISA requires every employer to retain records sufficient to determine benefits due (or which may become due) to employees covered by the employer's qualified plan and trust.

156.   This variety of obligations will cover a great many circumstances. Schedules supplying a balance sheet and income statement accounting information (and reconciling financial accounting books and records with the income tax return) are in any case submitted with corporate and partnership tax returns (and maintained by the IRS for at least six years in the case of partnerships and 75 years in the case of corporations). Furthermore, the non-tax rules applicable to trusts and the obligation of trustees require the maintenance of accounting records throughout the duration of the trust and for a period of time thereafter. However, although the rule under U.S. tax law provides that underlying documents must be maintained for so long as the contents thereof may become material in tax administration, an express rule requiring the maintenance of underlying documentation for five years is absent. While a balance sheet and income statement are reported to the IRS with each annual return, the consequences for choosing not to maintain other underlying accounting information will in some cases depend on the circumstances of that case. Where a taxpayer has claimed a deduction but is unable to substantiate the claim by producing the appropriate records, the deduction would be denied, and could be subject to substantial penalties. Should the IRS assert that income was earned, the taxpayer would have no means of rebutting that claim, and could also be subject to penalties. Consequently there is a gap in the United States' legal framework that could impede its ability to exchange information in certain limited cases.

157.   In practice, however, although two peers have cited some difficulties in obtaining accounting records none of them have indicated that the absence of an express five year rule is a problem. The IRS is also confident that the rules they have in place provide adequate incentives to maintain records for at least six years given the rules regarding substantial underreporting. However, where there is no reporting requirement for tax purposes, as may be the case of LLCs with a single owner, there may be no way of ensuring that adequate accounting records are available. There may also be limited circumstances where a trustee resident in the United States acting as the trustee of a foreign trust is not subject to any U.S. rules regarding the maintenance of accounting information, and any requirement to maintain accounting information may depend on foreign law (although the trustee would be subject to a U.S. court and the IRS summons power).

158.   In respect of the requirement that accounting records be maintained for at least 5 years, the United States should consider whether its federal income tax rules that require the maintenance of underlying documents for so long as the contents thereof may become material in tax administration ensure effective exchange of information. The U.S. should consider whether any refinements are necessary to its rules to ensure effective exchange of information in the limited cases where a trustee resident in the United States acting as the trustee of a foreign trust is not subject to any U.S. rules regarding the maintenance of accounting information. For LLCs with a single owner, the United States should ensure that such records are maintained.

Determination and factors underlying recommendations

Phase 1 Determination	
The element is in place, but certain aspects of the legal implementation of the element need improvement.	
Factors underlying recommendations	**Recommendations**
Accounting information for all single member LLCs is not always available.	The United States should ensure that accounting records (including underlying documentation) are available for all LLCs.

Phase 2 Rating
To be finalised as soon as a representative subset of Phase 2 reviews is completed.

A.3. Banking information

Banking information should be available for all account-holders.

Record-keeping requirements (ToR A.3. 1)

159.   The Currency and Foreign Transactions Reporting Act, commonly known as the Bank Secrecy Act (BSA), was enacted by the U.S. Congress in 1970 to establish requirements for recordkeeping and reporting by banks and a variety of other financial institutions and businesses and in some cases by individuals. The BSA generally requires financial institutions to assist government agencies detect and prevent money laundering and other related financial crimes (including tax evasion) by maintaining required records and filing reports.

160.   There is a requirement under the BSA that all such records required under the range of rules promulgated under Part 103 of the BSA must be retained for a period of at least five years from the date of the transaction (31 CFR §103.33). The specific records include:

- information regarding the purchaser and purchase transaction with respect to the issuance or sale of a bank check or draft, cashier's check, money order, or traveler's check for currency amounts between USD 3 000 and USD 10 000;

- a record of each extension of credit in an amount over USD 10 000, except when the extension is secured by an interest in real property;

- a record of each advice, request or instruction given or received regarding a transaction resulting in the transfer of funds, currency, checks, investment securities, other monetary instruments, investment securities, or credit, of more than USD 10 000, to or from any person, account or place outside the U.S.;

- a record of each advice, request or instruction given to another financial institution or other person located within or outside the U.S., regarding a transaction intended to result in a transfer of funds, currency, checks, investment securities, other monetary instruments or credit, of more than USD 10 000, to a person, account or place outside of the U.S.;

- the original or copy of each statement, ledger card or other record on each deposit or share account showing each transaction involving the account;

- the original or copy of each document granting signature authority over each deposit or customer account;

- the original or copy of each item (including checks, drafts, or transfers of credit) relating to a transaction of more than USD 10 000 remitted or transferred to a person, account or place outside the U.S.;

- the original or copy of each check or draft in an amount in excess of USD 10 000 drawn on or issued by a foreign bank which the domestic bank has paid or presented to a non-bank drawee for payment;

- each item relating to any transaction, including a record of each receipt of currency, other monetary instruments, checks, or investment securities and of each transfer of funds or credit, of more than USD 10 000 received on any one occasion directly and not through a domestic financial institution from a bank, broker or dealer in foreign exchange outside the U.S. or from any person, account or place outside of the U.S.;

- the original or copy of records prepared or received by a bank in the ordinary course of business which would be needed to reconstruct a demand deposit account and to trace a check in excess of USD 100 deposited in such demand deposit account through its domestic processing system or to supply a description of a deposited check in excess of USD 100;

- a record containing the name, address and taxpayer identification number, if available, of any person presenting a certificate of deposit for payment, as well as a description of the instrument and the date of the transaction;

- the original or copy of each deposit slip or credit ticket reflecting a transaction in excess of USD 100 or the equivalent record for direct deposit or other wire transfer deposit transaction including the amount of any currency involved;

- blotters, ledgers, or records of original entry regarding all purchases and sales of securities, all receipts and deliveries of securities, all receipts and disbursements of cash and all other debits and credits, with respect to cash and margin accounts; and

- a memorandum of each brokerage order, and of any other instruction, given or received for the purchase or sale of securities, whether executed or unexecuted, and copies of confirmations of all purchases and sales of securities.

161.   Regulations require that, as part of its customer identification program, a financial institution must collect (at a minimum) the following identifying information about a customer at the time the customer seeks to open the account: (1) name; (2) for individuals, date of birth; (3) for individuals, a residential or business street address, or, if there is no street address available, an Army Post Office or Fleet Post Office box number or the street address of next of kin or of another contact individual; or, for persons other than individuals, the principal place of business, local office or other physical location; and (4) for U.S. persons, a U.S. taxpayer identification number; or, for non-U.S. persons, one or more of the following: a U.S. taxpayer identification number, passport number and country of issuance; alien identification card number, or number and country of issuance of any other government-issued document evidencing nationality or residence and bearing a photograph or similar safeguard. In addition, the CIP must contain risk-based procedures for verifying each customer's identity. See, *e.g.* 31 C.F.R. § 103.121 (for banks), 31 § C.F.R. 103.122 (for broker-dealers); 31 C.F.R. § 103.123 (for FCMs); and 31 C.F.R. § 103.131 (for mutual funds).

162.   In its capacity as administrator of the BSA, FinCEN has authority to examine financial institutions and other businesses for compliance with the BSA

but has delegated this examination authority to other federal agencies. In the case of federally regulated financial institutions (banks, securities and futures firms and mutual funds), examination authority has been delegated to the federal regulators for the particular industry. These regulators supervise and examine the financial institutions that they regulate for compliance with applicable laws and regulations, including the BSA and its implementing regulations.

163.   The following numbers and types of depository institutions (all of which are defined as banks for the purposes of the BSA) were operating in the United States as of 31 December 2009:

(a) *1 462 Federal Deposit Insurance Corporation (FDIC)-insured nationally chartered commercial banks with USD 8.2 trillion total assets, which are all supervised by Office of the Comptroller of the Currency (OCC);*

(b) *844 FDIC-insured state chartered banks with USD 1.7 trillion total assets that are members of the Federal Reserve System, which are all supervised by the Federal Reserve;*

(c) *4 533 FDIC-insured state-chartered commercial and savings banks that are not members of the Federal Reserve with USD 1.9 trillion total assets, which are all supervised by the FDIC;*

(d) *1 173 FDIC-insured savings associations, with USD 1.3 trillion total assets, of which 765 are supervised by the Office of Thrift Supervision (OTS) and 408 are supervised by the FDIC; and*

(e) *10 978 credit unions (of which 7 554 are National Credit Union Administration (NCUA)- insured, federally chartered, and regulated by NCUA; and 3 424 are NCUA-insured, state-chartered, and regulated by state supervisory authorities; or privately insured and state-chartered and -regulated).*

164.   In addition, there are over 200 branches and agencies of foreign banks operating in the U.S., which are regulated by the Federal Reserve, the OCC, and/or the states.

Determination and factors underlying recommendations

Phase 1 Determination
The element is in place.

Phase 2 Rating
To be finalised as soon as a representative subset of Phase 2 reviews is completed

B. Access to Information

Overview

165.   A variety of information may be needed in a tax enquiry and jurisdictions should have the authority to obtain all such information. This includes information held by banks and other financial institutions as well as information concerning the ownership of companies or the identity of interest holders in other persons or entities, such as partnerships and trusts, as well as accounting information in respect of all such entities. This section of the report examines whether the United States' legal and regulatory framework gives the authorities access powers that cover all relevant people and information, and whether rights and safeguards are compatible with effective exchange of information. It also assesses the effectiveness of this framework in practice.

166.   The power of the IRS to obtain information for tax purposes is wide-ranging and is coupled with strong compulsory powers. Such powers are used regularly and the U.S. courts have been unequivocal in their view that these powers can be used to obtain information for the purpose of responding to a request for information under an information exchange mechanism. In the vast majority of requests for exchange-of-information assistance, the IRS does not rely on other U.S. governmental agencies to collect information necessary to respond to a request. The IRS most often is able to obtain the necessary information from its own records or from nongovernmental third parties. When a taxpayer or a third-party record keeper does not provide information voluntarily and it is necessary to issue and enforce a summons for information and documents, the IRS generally will seek judicial enforcement in collaboration with the U.S. Department of Justice. The IRS has a close working relationship with the U.S. Department of Justice, which has a long and successful record of enforcing IRS summonses with respect to both U.S. tax cases and foreign EOI requests.

167.   Bank information is confidential, and federal law generally prohibits disclosure of information to federal government authorities without notice to the customer and an opportunity for the customer to challenge the request.

However, there are numerous exceptions that work to assure the free flow of information to the government with respect to law enforcement procedures under federal income tax law, including where information is requested pursuant to an exchange of information agreement.

168.   Generally, U.S. law does not require the IRS to notify a taxpayer before providing to a DTC or TIEA partner information in the possession of the IRS, and taxpayers and third parties have no right to oppose or challenge the provision of information to a requesting party. Notice to the taxpayer is required in many cases when the IRS uses its compulsory summons authority to acquire information from third parties. Exceptions to this requirement exist in appropriate cases to ensure that it does not impede effective exchange of information.

B.1. Competent Authority's ability to obtain and provide information

> Competent authorities should have the power to obtain and provide information that is the subject of a request under an exchange of information arrangement from any person within their territorial jurisdiction who is in possession or control of such information (irrespective of any legal obligation on such person to maintain the secrecy of the information).

Bank, Ownership and identity information (ToR B.1.1)

169.   Under I.R.C. section 7602 *et seq.*, there are various tools available to secure requested information. A summons may be issued to examine books, papers, records, or other data of taxpayers and third parties and to obtain testimony under oath that may be relevant or material in ascertaining the correctness of any tax return, making a return where none has been made, determining a tax liability, collecting a tax liability, or inquiring into any offense connected with the administration or enforcement of the internal revenue laws. I.R.C. § 7602. The IRS may summon a taxpayer, an officer or employee of a taxpayer, a person having possession, custody, or care of the taxpayer's records, and any other person in possession of relevant and material evidence.

170.   As a step preliminary to exercising the formal summons authority, a revenue agent may in some instances first request the information through an information document request ("IDR") to the party in possession of the information. The IDR, although an official IRS request, does not carry the same compulsory force as a summons. If the agent believes greater compulsion is appropriate or necessary in light of the circumstances (including generally when information is requested from a bank), the agent will issue an administrative third-party summons for the information as an initial matter. Similarly, a summons will be issued if an IDR process is unsuccessful or complete information is not provided in response to an IDR. A summons

compels the person summoned to produce the records or testimony sought within a limited period (normally within a month's time). While in many instances the taxpayer identified in the summons (in addition to the person summoned) will be provided with notice of the summons within three days of the summons' service, the ability to pose a legal challenge to the summons are quite narrowly drawn. See sections B.1.3 and B.2, below.

171.   The summons power, and other powers of inspection, are held directly by the IRS; the IRS Deputy Commissioner (International), in his capacity as the U.S. Competent Authority, has power to obtain information directly using revenue agents and officers under his chain of authority and also in other branches of the IRS. The IRS, including the U.S. Competent Authority, exercises its powers directly and does not need to invoke special procedures, whether administrative, judicial or otherwise, to exercise such powers effectively. In some situations where the IRS has issued an administrative summons, the IRS may choose to bring judicial action to enforce the summons if the party summoned does not comply, and the taxpayer in some situations may initiate a judicial proceeding to quash the summons; see I.R.C. § 7609.

172.   Information collected for anti-money laundering purposes in the United States would ordinarily be kept by FinCEN, a separate bureau of the Department of the Treasury. The IRS has access to such information for law enforcement purposes, including tax investigation purposes and this information may be provided by the IRS in response to a request for exchange of information. Specifically, 31 C.F.R. § 103.53(b) provides that "the Secretary may make any information set forth in any report received pursuant to this part available to another agency of the United States, to an agency of a state or local government or to an agency of a foreign government, upon the request of the head of such department or agency made in writing and stating the particular information desired, the criminal, tax or regulatory purpose for which the information is sought, and the official need for the information". In practice, by memorandum of agreement with FinCEN, the IRS maintains the information technology and systems that hold the information regarding Foreign Bank Account Reports.

173.   In the vast majority of requests for exchange-of-information assistance, the IRS does not rely on other U.S. governmental agencies to collect information necessary to respond to a request. The IRS most often is able to obtain the necessary information from its own records or from nongovernmental third parties. When a taxpayer or a third-party record keeper does not provide information voluntarily and it is necessary to issue and enforce a summons for information and documents, the IRS generally will seek judicial enforcement in collaboration with the U.S. Department of Justice, which will represent the Commissioner of the IRS in a judicial enforcement proceeding brought before a federal district court judge. The IRS has a close working

relationship with the U.S. Department of Justice, which has a long and successful record of enforcing IRS summonses with respect to both U.S. tax cases and foreign EOI requests.

174.   In the less-common instances where information is held by another government agency at the federal, state, or local level, the IRS will seek the information in the same manner and to the same extent that it does in U.S. cases. The Office of Governmental Liaison (GL), within the IRS, is responsible for partnering with federal, state, and local governmental agencies on initiatives that improve tax administration at all levels of government.

175.   The primary state and local agencies with which GL manages relationships are the state and local taxing and employment agencies, such as departments of revenue and employment (workforce) agencies. The IRS has information sharing arrangements with each of the states. These agreements include specific memoranda of understanding or other written agreements with many of these agencies that allow the exchange of federal tax information. Agreements are also in place with many non-tax federal, state and local agencies. Under the agreements with IRS, certain information is shared on a recurring basis, such as monthly, quarterly, or annually. It should be noted, however, that such agreements are not required for the IRS to be able to obtain information on request from state and local taxing and employment agencies, or from any other federal, state or local agency.

176.   There are no materially different processes involved when a request relates to a criminal investigation case as compared to a civil examination. Requests for EOI assistance relating to foreign criminal tax investigations are processed with the assistance of special agents in the Criminal Investigation Division of the IRS, who have specialized knowledge and training for gathering relevant evidence to support a criminal tax case.

177.   With respect to the IRS's ability to obtain information using compulsory means, the IRS's broad summons authority applies to both civil and criminal tax cases. In civil cases, notice to taxpayers described in a summons to a third party is often required.[10] By contrast, in criminal cases the requirement to give notice to taxpayers listed in a summons is more circumscribed. See I.R.C. § 7609(c)(2).

---

10.   Even where notice is otherwise required, in both civil and criminal cases the IRS may apply to a federal district court for a determination that excuses the IRS from notifying the taxpayer and third parties named in the summons where there is reasonable cause to believe that the giving of notice may lead to attempts to conceal, destroy, or alter records relevant to the examination, to prevent the communication of information through intimidation, bribery, or collusion, or to flee to avoid prosecution, testifying, or production of records. See I.R.C. § 7609(g).

178.   All information obtained from taxpayers or third parties having possession or control of the information is reviewed to ensure that the information received is responsive and complete. The information obtained from a taxpayer/record keeper is (1) reviewed by the audit team/field personnel that obtained the information (when field resources are utilized) and/or (2) reviewed by the Competent Authority/Exchange of Information office personnel who are responsible for providing the information to the jurisdiction making the request. These steps are performed before the response is prepared and sent to the requesting country. If information is missing, the IRS will revert to the taxpayer/record keeper and inform them that they are not excused from the IRS IDR/summons because the information supplied is not fully responsive to the request.

Accounting records (ToR B.1.2)

179.   The powers described above apply equally in the case of accounting records.

Use of information gathering measures absent domestic tax interest (ToR B.1.3)

180.   The powers held by the IRS to obtain information can be used to respond to a request for exchange of information in tax matters regardless of whether the IRS has any need for the information for their own tax purposes. To be valid and enforceable, any summons must (a) seek information that may be relevant to the investigation, (b) be issued pursuant to a proper purpose, (c) seek information that the IRS does not already possess, and (d) comply with administrative steps required in the Internal Revenue Code. U.S. v. Powell, 379 U.S. 48 (1964).

181.   A summons enforcement proceeding initiated on behalf of a foreign tax authority under a tax treaty that meets the statutory requirements and is issued in good faith is valid and enforceable. U.S. v. Stuart, 489 U.S. 353 (1989); Lidas v. U.S., 238 F.3d 1076 (9th Cir. 2001). Summons enforcement has also been upheld in court for requests under TIEAs. Zarate Barquero v. U.S., 18 F.3d 1311 (5th Cir. 1994). An affidavit of the U.S. Competent Authority can be used to establish a prima facie case under the four-factor test in *Powell* for enforcement of an IRS summons; the legitimate purpose requirement is met by the need to efficiently fulfil the USA's obligations under the tax treaty. Mazurek v. U.S., 271 F.3d 226 (5th Cir. 2001). The courts have rejected arguments that a summons was unenforceable because it would not be permissible under the law of the foreign country, because the foreign investigation is not an ongoing tax investigation for this purpose, or because the court should be required to examine the request from the foreign tax authority. See, *e.g.* Azouz v. U.S., 1999 U.S. Dist. LEXIS 21396 (S.D.N.Y.);

Fernandez-Marinelli v. U.S., 1995 U.S. Dist. LEXIS 17695 (S.D.N.Y.); U.S. v. Hiley, 2007 WL 2904056 (S.D. Cal. 2007).

Compulsory powers (ToR B.1.4)

182.   If any person is summoned under the internal revenue laws to appear, to testify, or to produce books, papers, records, or other data, the United States District Court for the district in which such person resides or is found has jurisdiction by appropriate process to compel compliance. See I.R.C. §§ 7604, 7609. Conviction for failure to comply with an administrative summons is punishable by a fine of up to USD 1 000 or a prison sentence of up to 1 year, or both, together with the costs of prosecution. I.R.C. § 7210. Also, in the event that a summoned party does not comply with a U.S. court's order to produce, the U.S. court has inherent powers (under U.S. common law) to impose so-called "civil contempt" sanctions, *i.e.* daily imposition of fines and/or incarceration, until the summoned person complies with the court's enforcement order. See B.1.5 for citations to and a brief description of a few such cases.

183.   More generally, any person required to pay any tax, or required to make a return (including information returns), keep any records, or supply any information, who wilfully fails to pay such tax, make such return, keep such records, or supply such information, at the time or times required by law or regulations, shall, in addition to other penalties provided by law, be guilty of a misdemeanor and, upon conviction thereof, be fined not more than USD 25 000 (USD 100 000 in the case of a corporation) or imprisoned not more than 1 year, or both, together with the costs of prosecution. I.R.C. § 7203.

184.   In addition, certain classes of entities are subject to additional specific penalties for failure to comply with a summons. For example, a "reporting corporation" subject to the rules of I.R.C. section 6038A or I.R.C. section 6038C (25% foreign-owned or engaged in U.S. trade or business) is subject to a special civil penalty adjustment for failure to comply with an administrative summons for information relating to a transaction with a foreign related party. In the event of such a failure, the IRS may use its discretion and the limited information then in its possession to determine the federal tax treatment of the transaction. I.R.C. §§ 6038A(e), 6038C(d). The IRS is empowered more generally to determine the federal tax treatment of a transaction in the absence of appropriate information (including the provision of false information) by filing a return for the taxpayer. I.R.C. §6020(b).

Secrecy provisions (ToR B.1.5)

185.   The confidentiality of bank account information is generally defined and delimited by the Right to Financial Privacy Act (RFPA), 12 U.S.C. § 3401-22. This statute, enacted in 1978, generally prohibits disclosure of

information to federal government authorities without notice to the customer and an opportunity for the customer to challenge the request. However, there are numerous exceptions that work to assure the free flow of information to the government with respect to law enforcement. Perhaps the broadest area carved out of the applicability of the RFPA is tax enforcement; 12 U.S.C. § 3413(c) permits disclosure of financial records under enforcement procedures in Title 26 of the United States Code (the Internal Revenue Code), including summons procedures undertaken in order to respond to a request for information under an international agreement.

186.   The most commonly used procedure for obtaining financial records from banks for federal tax purposes is the administrative summons procedure authorized by I.R.C. sections 7602 and 7609. The RFPA contains a specific exception to its confidentiality rules in respect of the disclosure of financial information where "such financial records are disclosed in response to an administrative subpoena or summons" (§ 3402). Where a non-resident has an account with a U.S. bank, the confidentiality requirements of the RFPA would not prevent the IRS from obtaining information in regard to that account under its normal procedure for obtaining bank information. There is no requirement that the US be provided the name of the account-holder in order to obtain bank information in respect of that person, but, as a practical matter, sufficient identifying information (for example an account number or a tax identification number) will be required in order to fulfill the request. Additionally, in circumstances where the information otherwise represents an appropriate information exchange request, information regarding an ascertainable class of account holders that can be identified with specificity can be obtained. A number of peers indicated that they have had some difficulty in practice obtaining bank information, and in particular noted the long processing times (see discussion in section C.5, below). The U.S. indicates that they are introducing measures to help ensure timely responses, including ways to make the summons procedure more efficient.Finally, 12 U.S.C. § 3413(k) authorizes the disclosure of the names and addresses of account holders to the Treasury Department for purposes of withholding taxes on non-resident aliens.

187.   Law enforcement and other competent authorities have the power to compel production of financial records through the issuance of administrative, grand jury or civil subpoenas. Law enforcement authorities can conduct searches of persons or premises to obtain evidence of financial crimes, including the seizure of financial documents, if a search warrant is obtained from an appropriate judicial authority or where there are exigent circumstances which negate the necessity of obtaining a search warrant. The documents obtained through the issuance of subpoenas or obtained through searches can be used in the investigation and prosecution of various financial crimes. Search and seizure powers are available for the investigation of all crimes (including, but not limited to, tax and financial crimes). The RFPA,

although generally prohibiting disclosure of information to federal government authorities without notice to the customer and an opportunity for the customer to challenge the request, provides exceptions in the context of administrative, grand jury or civil subpoenas or, most notably, any enforcement procedure under the Internal Revenue Code. In addition, criminal and civil penalties exist for notifying a person whose records have been subpoenaed. 18 U.S.C. § 1510(b) (criminal fines and prison terms of up to five years); 12 U.S.C. § 3420(b) (RFPA civil penalties for disclosure).

188.   The attorney-client privilege rule under U.S. law preserves confidential communications between attorneys and their clients that are disclosed for the purpose of furnishing or obtaining legal advice or assistance. Generally, the rule provides that a communication made in confidence by a client is privileged where legal advice of any kind is sought from a professional legal adviser in his capacity as such and the communication relates to that purpose. Where the advice sought from the legal professional is not legal advice but, for example, accounting advice, the privilege does not apply. U.S. courts have found that,"[a] ttorney-client privilege does not apply to communications between a client and an attorney where the attorney is employed in a non-legal capacity, for instance as an accountant, escrow agency, negotiator, or notary public." See Harlandale Independent School District v. Cornyn, 25 S.W.3d 328, 332 (Tex. App. 2000). To the extent, therefore, that an attorney acts as a nominee shareholder, a trustee, a settlor, a company director or under a power of attorney to represent a company in its business affairs, exchange of information resulting from and relating to any such activity cannot be declined because of the attorney-client privilege rule. In addition, communications are not privileged when communications between an attorney and client are used to further a crime or fraud.

189.   With limited exception, the United States attorney-client privilege does not extend to communications between a client and a third party who is not an attorney. A limited rule applies to certain expert third parties, such as accountants, when such persons are engaged by the attorney to assist in connection with (or in contemplation of) legal proceedings. This exception is narrowly drawn by case law and only applies where the assistance of the expert is essential to the provision of the legal advice. In Kovel the court observed that "[w]hat is vital to the privilege is that the communication be made in confidence for the purpose of obtaining legal advice from the lawyer. If what is sought is not legal advice but only accounting service, as in Olender v. United States, 210 F.2d 795, 805-806 (9th Cir. 1954), see Reisman v. Caplin, 61-2 U.S.T.C. P9673 (1961), or if the advice sought is the accountant's rather than the lawyer's, no privilege exists." See Kovel v. United States, 296 F.2d 918 (2d Cir. 1961).

Determination and factors underlying recommendations

Phase 1 Determination
The element is in place.

Phase 2 Rating
To be finalised as soon as a representative subset of Phase 2 reviews is completed

B.2. Notification requirements and rights and safeguards

The rights and safeguards (*e.g.* notification, appeal rights) that apply to persons in the requested jurisdiction should be compatible with effective exchange of information.

Not unduly prevent or delay exchange of information (ToR B.2.1)

190. Generally, U.S. law does not require the IRS to notify a taxpayer before providing to a DTC or TIEA partner information in the possession of the IRS, and taxpayers and third parties have no right to oppose or challenge the provision of information to a requesting party. Tax administration generally is an express exception to the rule under the Right to Financial Privacy Act (RFPA) prohibiting disclosure of information to federal government authorities without notice to the customer, and criminal and civil penalties exist for notifying a person whose records have been subpoenaed. 18 U.S.C. § 1510(b) (criminal fines and prison terms of up to five years); 12 U.S.C. § 3420(b) (RFPA civil penalties for disclosure).

191. Notice to the taxpayer is required in many cases when the IRS uses its compulsory summons authority (as opposed to an IDR) to acquire information from third parties. I.R.C. § 7602(c)(1). In particular, a copy of each IRS summons generally must be mailed to the taxpayer. I.R.C. § 7609. Exceptions to this requirement exist for certain types of information sought in criminal cases, or where a court order is obtained upon showing there is reasonable cause to believe the giving of notice may lead to attempts to conceal, destroy, or alter records relevant to the examination, to prevent the communication of information by other persons through intimidation, bribery, or collusion, or to flee to avoid prosecution, testifying, or production of records.

192. Any person who is entitled to notice of a summons has the right to petition (within 20 days of service) a federal court to "quash" the summons. The grounds for quashing an IRS summons are narrowly drawn under U.S. law. In determining whether a summons is enforceable, courts focus on whether (1) the summons was issued pursuant to a legitimate purpose,

(2) the information sought in the summons is relevant to that purpose, (3) the information is not already within the IRS's possession, and (4) the administrative steps required by the Internal Revenue Code have been followed. (See discussion above under section B.1 regarding the requirements for a valid summons.)

193.   When information is already in possession of the IRS, and after information is obtained by the IRS from third parties, whether pursuant to a voluntary request or a summons, the IRS is not required to notify taxpayers or third parties that the information will be transmitted to a DTC or TIEA partner. Notice to the taxpayer is required in various cases where the IRS uses its compulsory summons authority (as opposed to an IDR) to acquire information from third parties. I.R.C. § 7602(c)(1). Exceptions to the notification requirement associated with the exercise of summons authority exist for certain types of information sought in criminal cases, or where a court order is obtained upon showing there is reasonable cause to believe that giving notice may lead to attempts to conceal, destroy, or alter records relevant to the examination, to prevent the communication of information by other persons through intimidation, bribery, or collusion, or to flee to avoid prosecution, testifying, or production of records.

Limitations on financial privacy rights

194.   Confidentiality of bank account information is generally defined and delimited by the Right to Financial Privacy Act (RFPA), 12 U.S.C. §§ 3401-22, enacted in 1978. This statute generally prohibits disclosure of information to federal government authorities without notice to the customer and an opportunity for the customer to challenge the request. However, there are numerous exceptions that work to assure the free flow of information to the government with respect to law enforcement.

195.   Perhaps the broadest area carved out of the applicability of the RFPA is tax enforcement; 12 U.S.C. § 3413(c) permits disclosure of financial records under enforcement procedures in Title 26 of the United States Code (the Internal Revenue Code). The legal regime used by U.S. tax authorities to obtain information from banks for a requesting state, which consist principally of the administrative summons power, is part of the IRS's routine administrative information gathering powers included in Title 26 of the United States Code (codified at I.R.C. section 7602 *et seq.*). This same regime is routinely used to obtain information from banks for domestic tax matters. The IRS, including the U.S. Competent Authority, exercises its powers directly and does not need to invoke special procedures, whether administrative, judicial or otherwise, to obtain information from banks.

196.   The RFPA also generally does not apply to information subject to a grand jury subpoena. Accordingly, when a grand jury subpoena is used to obtain the financial records of a customer from a financial institution, the Department of Justice is not required by the RFPA to give any notice to the customer or provide certification of RFPA compliance to the financial institution. Criminal and civil penalties exist for notifying a person whose records have been subpoenaed. 18 U.S.C. § 1510(b)(criminal fines and prison term of up to five years); and 12 U.S.C. § 3420(b) (RFPA civil penalties for disclosure). The grand jury subpoena exception to the RFPA is an additional, freestanding exception to the RFPA, largely unrelated to the RFPA exception for tax enforcement. Because EOI requests (including for bank account information otherwise generally protected by the RFPA) are effectively addressed through the administrative summons power under U.S. tax law, the IRS does not use grand jury subpoenas in this way. Such subpoenas traditionally are used to inquire into criminal violations of U.S. law. Whether information is obtained by the IRS via administrative summons or in the grand jury process via subpoena, similar exceptions from notice requirements apply. See I.R.C. sections 7609(c)(3) and 7609(g); 12 U.S.C. 3413(i) and 3409(a).

Determination and factors underlying recommendations

Phase 1 Determination
The element is in place.

Phase 2 Rating
To be finalised as soon as a representative subset of Phase 2 reviews is completed

C. Exchanging Information

Overview

197.   Jurisdictions generally cannot exchange information for tax purposes unless they have a legal basis or mechanisms for doing so. A jurisdiction's practical capacity to effectively exchange information relies both on having adequate mechanisms in place as well as an adequate institutional framework. This section of the report assesses the United States' network of EOI agreements against the standards and the adequacy of its institutional framework to achieve effective exchange of information in practice.

198.   The United States has an extensive network of exchange of information agreements that meet the international standards and that cover all relevant partners. Requirements for confidentiality and the maintenance of rights and safeguards are in place.

199.   The United States processes a very large number of information requests each year in addition to a program of both spontaneous and automatic exchange as well as simultaneous tax examinations and simultaneous criminal tax investigations. The United States was a founding member of the Joint International Tax Shelter Information Centre and actively participates in the exchange of information with its other members. The exchange of information unit within the IRS is generally well-trained and well-organised. Tax attachés in offices around the world facilitate exchange of information in certain key geographic areas. Guidelines for the exchange of information provide for specific timelines in which EOI requests should be processed, including the provision of interim requests in complex cases.

200.   The IRS deals with requests for all types of information. The United States' information exchange partners have indicated that they have a very positive relationship with the United States on information exchange and are generally very satisfied. For the combined review period, the United States reports that it fully responded within 90 days to more than 50% of specific requests (51%), within 180 days to more than 75% of specific requests (76%), and within 365 days to more than 90% of specific requests (91%). This is

generally consistent with the information provided by the peers. Specific issues have been raised regarding the availability of information in certain cases, and with the time required to process requests, in particular with regard to requests for banking information. The United States should examine how its competent authority could speed up its internal processes for obtaining and providing information to ensure more timely responses and provide a status update within 90 days in all cases. The IRS reports that, based on data analyzed in preparation for its peer review, and the recommendations of the assessors, it is making changes to its internal processes to further improve its responsiveness to requests and ensure it has a process to provide regular status updates.

C.1. Exchange-of-information mechanisms

> Exchange of information mechanisms should allow for effective exchange of information.

201. The United States has signed agreements for the exchange of information in tax matters that meet the standards with 77 jurisdictions. These include 53 double taxation conventions (DTCs) and 24 tax information exchange agreements (TIEAs).

202. The United States negotiates its DTCs based on a US model convention. The model convention contains an exchange of information provision that is virtually identical to the analogous provisions in the OECD and UN model tax conventions. Article 26 (Exchange of Information and Administrative Assistance) of the US Model Income Tax Convention 2006 reads:

> *1. The competent authorities of the Contracting States shall exchange such information as may be relevant for carrying out the provisions of this Convention or of the domestic laws of the Contracting States concerning taxes of every kind imposed by a Contracting State to the extent that the taxation thereunder is not contrary to the Convention, including information relating to the assessment or collection of, the enforcement or prosecution in respect of, or the determination of appeals in relation to, such taxes. The exchange of information is not restricted by paragraph 1 of Article 1 (General Scope) or Article 2 (Taxes Covered).*
>
> *2. Any information received under this Article by a Contracting State shall be treated as secret in the same manner as information obtained under the domestic laws of that State and shall be disclosed only to persons or authorities (including courts and administrative bodies) involved in the assessment, collection, or administration of, the enforcement or prosecution in respect of, or the determination of*

appeals in relation to, the taxes referred to above, or the oversight of such functions. Such persons or authorities shall use the information only for such purposes. They may disclose the information in public court proceedings or in judicial decisions.

3. In no case shall the provisions of the preceding paragraphs be construed so as to impose on a Contracting State the obligation:

a) to carry out administrative measures at variance with the laws and administrative practice of that or of the other Contracting State;

b) to supply information that is not obtainable under the laws or in the normal course of the administration of that or of the other Contracting State;

c) to supply information that would disclose any trade, business, industrial, commercial, or professional secret or trade process, or information the disclosure of which would be contrary to public policy (ordre public).

4. If information is requested by a Contracting State in accordance with this Article, the other Contracting State shall use its information gathering measures to obtain the requested information, even though that other State may not need such information for its own purposes. The obligation contained in the preceding sentence is subject to the limitations of paragraph 3 but in no case shall such limitation be construed to permit a Contracting State to decline to supply information because it has no domestic interest in such information.

5. In no case shall the provisions of paragraph 3 be construed to permit a Contracting State to decline to supply information requested by the other Contracting State because the information is held by a bank, other financial institution, nominee or person acting in an agency or a fiduciary capacity or because it relates to ownership interests in a person.

203.   The U.S. model deviates from the OECD and UN models in that the scope of exchange relates to information that "may be relevant" to the administration of tax laws, rather than "foreseeably relevant". However, the phrase used in the U.S. model mandates an exchange of information that is at least as wide as, and arguably wider than, the international standards require (see discussion under C.1.1). In addition, the U.S. model in paragraphs 4 and 5 omit the word "solely" before "because". This phrasing broadens the scope of exchange.

204.   Many of the TIEAs entered into by the United States pre-date the development of the OECD model agreement on exchange of information on tax matters published in 2002. These TIEAs – with the exception of the TIEA with Costa Rica (signed in 1989) – also provide for exchange of information on request in

accordance with the standards. The TIEA with Costa Rica restricts the exchange of bank information to cases of tax fraud as defined under Costa Rican law.

Foreseeably relevant standard (ToR C.1.1)

205. The language of the US Model Income Tax Convention refers to information that "may be relevant" for carrying out the provisions of domestic tax law. The model is accompanied by a Technical Explanation, which elaborates on the meaning of "may be relevant":

> *The information to be exchanged is that which may be relevant for carrying out the provisions of the Convention or the domestic laws of the United States or of the other Contracting State concerning taxes of every kind applied at the national level. This language incorporates the standard in 26 U.S.C. Section 7602 which authorizes the IRS to examine "any books, papers, records, or other data which may be relevant or material." (Emphasis added.) In United States v. Arthur Young & Co., 465 U.S. 805, 814 (1984), the Supreme Court stated that the language "may be" reflects Congress's express intention to allow the IRS to obtain "items of even potential relevance to an ongoing investigation, without reference to its admissibility."*

206. All of the United States' EOI agreements allow for the exchange of information that meet the foreseeably relevant standard.

207. It should also be noted that the USA-Bermuda TIEA is restricted on its face to providing assistance relating to the prevention of tax fraud and the evasion of taxes. The competent authorities of those jurisdictions have entered in an agreement as provided for in the TIEA that expands the scope of exchange to information that is foreseeably relevant to the administration of tax laws. This agreement has been in effect for over 10 years.

In respect of all persons (ToR C.1.2)

208. All of the United States' EOI agreements allow for the exchange of information in respect of all persons.

Obligation to exchange all types of information (ToR C.1.3)

209. Jurisdictions cannot engage in effective exchange of information if they cannot exchange information held by financial institutions, nominees or persons acting in an agency or a fiduciary capacity. Article 26(5) of the OECD Model Tax Convention provides that a contracting state may not decline to supply information because the information is held by a bank, other financial

institution, nominee or person acting in an agency or a fiduciary capacity or because it relates to ownership interests in a person. However, the absence of this paragraph does not automatically create restrictions on exchange of bank information. The commentary on article 26(5) indicates that while paragraph 5, added to the Model Tax Convention in 2005, represents a change in the structure of the Article, it should not be interpreted as suggesting that the previous version of the Article did not authorise the exchange of such information. The United States has access to bank information for tax purposes and is able to exchange this type of information when requested on a reciprocal basis irrespective of whether its agreements contain the equivalent of Article 26(5).

210.   The terms of the United States-Costa Rica TIEA limits the exchange of bank information to cases of tax fraud as defined under Costa Rican law. The United States' DTC with Austria does not contain a provision that expressly requires the exchange of bank information equivalent to paragraph 5 of the US model. Given limitations on the exchange of bank information in Austria, and the reciprocity conditions of the agreement, the DTC does not generally allow for the exchange of this type of information. It should be noted, however, that the limitations with Costa Rica and Austria reflect limitations inherent in the laws of those jurisdictions, and not on limitations on the internal laws of the U.S. to obtain said information. The policy of the United States is to negotiate tax information exchange consistent with international standards, and as the policy of other jurisdictions changes, the United States policy is to renegotiate TIEAs and DTCs accordingly.

Absence of domestic tax interest (ToR C.1.4)

211.   The concept of a "domestic tax interest" describes a situation where a contracting party can only provide information to another contracting party if it has an interest in the requested information for its own tax purposes. An inability to provide information based on a domestic tax interest requirement is not consistent with the international standard. Contracting parties must use their information gathering measures even though invoked solely to obtain and provide information to the other contracting party.

212.   All of the United States' EOI agreements allow for the exchange of information absent a domestic tax interest. There is no limitation in the United States' domestic law that prevents exchange of information absent a domestic tax interest. There may be restrictions in some of the U.S.'s partner jurisdictions that have not yet been reviewed by the Global Forum.

Absence of dual criminality principles (ToR C.1.5)

213.   The United States-Costa Rica TIEA requires that bank information can only be exchanged where the case involves tax fraud as defined under

Costa Rican law. The rest of the EOI agreements concluded by the U.S. do not apply the dual criminality principle to restrict the exchange of information.

Exchange of information in both civil and criminal tax matters (ToR C.1.6)

214.   All of the United States' EOI agreements allow for exchange of information in both civil and criminal tax matters.

Provide information in specific form requested (ToR C.1.7)

215.   All of the United States' EOI agreements require the requested jurisdiction to provide information in the specific form requested, to the extent that such form is known and permitted under the requested jurisdictions laws. In addition, many of the United States' TIEAs include requirements that information be provided in specific enumerated forms (such as deposition of witnesses). Under U.S. law information can be obtained in a variety of particular forms, such as the authenticated copy of an original document or in the form of a deposition of a witness).

In force (ToR C.1.8)

216.   The United States signed protocols in 2009 to update the information exchange provisions of its existing agreements with both Switzerland and Luxembourg. In 2010 the United States signed a DTC with Chile, and also signed the protocol to the Joint Council of Europe/OECD Convention on Mutual Administrative Assistance in Tax Matters. These agreements have not yet been ratified by the US Senate.

In effect (ToR C.1.9)

217.   The United States' has enacted the laws necessary to give effect to its EOI agreements.

Determination and factors underlying recommendations

Phase 1 Determination
The element is in place.

Phase 2 Rating
To be finalised as soon as a representative subset of Phase 2 reviews is completed

C.2. Exchange-of-information mechanisms with all relevant partners

> The jurisdictions' network of information exchange mechanisms should cover all relevant partners.

218.   Ultimately, the international standard requires that jurisdictions exchange information with all relevant partners, meaning those partners who are interested in entering into an information exchange arrangement. Agreements cannot be concluded only with counterparties without economic significance. If it appears that a jurisdiction is refusing to enter into agreements or negotiations with partners, in particular ones that have a reasonable expectation of requiring information from that jurisdiction in order to properly administer and enforce its tax laws it may indicate a lack of commitment to implement the standards.

219.   The United States has a wide network of EOI agreements (53 DTCs and 24 TIEAs) and are actively negotiating further agreements. The existing network includes agreements with almost all OECD and G20 countries and covers the United States' major trading partners (Canada, China, Mexico, Japan, Germany and the United Kingdom). The United States was one of the first countries to conclude tax information exchange agreements, which it began negotiating in the 1980s, in particular with Caribbean and South American jurisdictions. Consequently, the United States has one of the widest network of TIEAs.

220.   No peer jurisdiction has indicated that the United States has been unwilling to negotiate an EOI agreement. Multiple jurisdictions have approached the US to negotiate information exchange agreements, and the United States is actively negotiating both TIEAs and DTCs.

Determination and factors underlying recommendations

Phase 1 Determination	
The element is in place.	
Factors underlying recommendations	**Recommendations**
	The United States should continue to develop its EOI network with all relevant partners.

Phase 2 Rating
To be finalised as soon as a representative subset of Phase 2 reviews is completed

C.3. Confidentiality

> The jurisdictions' mechanisms for exchange of information should have adequate provisions to ensure the confidentiality of information received.

Information received: disclosure, use, and safeguards (ToR C.3.1)

221. U.S. tax treaties and TIEAs typically include a provision substantially similar to the following provision from Article 26 of the U.S. Model Income Tax Convention, which is also substantially similar to Article 26, paragraph 2 of the OECD Model:

> *Any information received under this Article by a Contracting State shall be treated as secret in the same manner as information obtained under the domestic laws of that State and shall be disclosed only to persons or authorities (including courts and administrative bodies) involved in the assessment, collection, or administration of, the enforcement or prosecution in respect of, or the determination of appeals in relation to, the taxes [covered by the Convention], or the oversight of such functions. Such persons or authorities shall use the information only for such purposes. They may disclose the information in public court proceedings or in judicial decisions.*

222. The United States strictly observes its domestic confidentiality laws. I.R.C. section 6103 generally protects the confidentiality of tax-return information, including taxpayer-specific information received from another country under an exchange-of-information mechanism. There are a limited number of well-defined exceptions to the general rule of confidentiality.

223. I.R.C. section 6105 provides generally that information exchanged pursuant to a tax convention may not be disclosed. For this purpose, a tax convention includes not only a tax treaty but also any bilateral or multilateral agreement providing for the avoidance of double taxation, the prevention of fiscal evasion, non-discrimination with respect to taxes, the exchange of tax-relevant information with the United States, or mutual assistance in tax matters.

224. I.R.C. section 6103 contains a limited number of well-defined exceptions to the general rule of confidentiality. For example, the taxpayer's own information generally may be disclosed to the taxpayer unless it is determined that such disclosure would seriously impair federal tax administration. Taxpayer information may be disclosed to a foreign competent authority pursuant to a tax treaty or similar agreement, or under certain conditions to the Department of Justice or for use in a judicial tax proceeding. Similarly, under U.S. tax treaties and TIEAs and under I.R.C. section 6105, information received pursuant to an information exchange request may be disclosed to

persons or authorities (including courts and administrative bodies) involved in the assessment, collection, or administration of, the enforcement or prosecution in respect of, or the determination of appeals in relation to, the taxes covered by the tax treaty or TIEA, including the oversight of such taxes by certain governmental bodies. Such persons or authorities shall use the information only for such purposes. They may disclose the information in public court proceedings or in judicial decisions. Where such information does not relate to a particular taxpayer, it may be disclosed if the competent authority determines, after consultation with each other party to the tax convention(s), that the disclosure would not impair tax administration.

225. Where a communication is made between jurisdictions pursuant to a tax treaty or TIEA, the communication is generally protected by the confidentiality provisions of the treaty or TIEA and by the confidentiality provisions of domestic law on the same basis as information requested under the tax treaty or TIEA.

226. Violation of U.S. confidentiality laws with respect to tax information is punishable by both criminal and civil penalties. Wilful unauthorized disclosure of returns or return information is a felony punishable by a fine of up to USD 5 000 or imprisonment of up to 5 years, or both. I.R.C. § 7213. These penalties apply not only against the government employee who committed the unauthorized disclosure but also against a person who receives the information and knowingly publishes it. In addition, wilful unauthorized access to or inspection of returns or return information is a misdemeanor punishable by a fine of up to USD 1 000 or imprisonment of up to 1 year, or both. I.R.C. § 7213A. A federal employee convicted of any of these crimes is discharged from employment. The taxpayer may bring a civil action for damages under I.R.C. section 7431 for any wilful or negligent unauthorized disclosure of a return or return information. Damages payable in such civil actions are the greater of USD 1 000 for each act of disclosure or actual damages sustained (increased by punitive damages in cases of wilful or gross negligence). The plaintiff may also collect court costs. All of these penalties potentially apply as well to unauthorized disclosure of return information received pursuant to a tax treaty or TIEA information exchange request in violation of I.R.C. section 6105.

227. The confidentiality of information is taken very seriously and, as a general matter, information held by the IRS is only available on a need to know basis. Systems are in place to protect against unauthorised access and violations are dealt with when they do occur. The IRS goes to great lengths to ensure that material related to exchange of information is only accessible by those persons involved in the exchange of information process. There have not been any cases where information received by the U.S. Competent authority from an EOI partner has been made public other than in accordance with

the terms under the DTC/TIEA exchange-of-information provisions. Pursuant to federal law, including the exchange-of-information provisions of tax treaties, the IRS treats taxpayer information (including information received from treaty/TIEA partners) as confidential. A number of government publications describe in detail the confidentiality obligations of taxpayer information generally as well as specific rules pertaining to information obtained under a treaty or through interactions with foreign tax officials. Administrative procedures, rules and regulations are clearly described to ensure that information exchanged pursuant to EOI arrangements or received from foreign tax authorities is treated as confidential and that any disclosure is strictly in accordance with the relevant exchange of information agreement.

All other information exchanged (ToR C.3.2)

228.   The provisions discussed above regarding confidentiality of information exchanged pursuant to an information exchange agreement apply equally to the information provided in response to a request as well as all other information exchanged in the process.

Determination and factors underlying recommendations

Phase 1 Determination
The element is in place.

Phase 2 Rating
To be finalised as soon as a representative subset of Phase 2 reviews is completed

C.4. Rights and safeguards of taxpayers and third parties

The exchange of information mechanisms should respect the rights and safeguards of taxpayers and third parties.

Exceptions to requirement to provide information (ToR C.4.1.)

229.   U.S. tax treaties and TIEAs typically include a provision substantially similar to the following provision from Article 26 of the U.S. Model Income Tax Convention, which is also substantially similar to Article 26, paragraph 3 of the OECD Model:

> In no case shall [Article 26] be construed so as to impose on a Contracting State the obligation:

a) to carry out administrative measures at variance with the laws and administrative practice of that or of the other Contracting State;

b) to supply information that is not obtainable under the laws or in the normal course of the administration of that or of the other Contracting State;

c) to supply information that would disclose any trade, business, industrial, commercial, or professional secret or trade process, or information the disclosure of which would be contrary to public policy (ordre public).

230.   Confidentiality with respect to attorney-client communications is one of several privileges protected by common law in the United States. Under the quoted provision of Article 26, because such material is not obtainable under the laws of the United States or in the normal course of its adminis-tration, the United States may appropriately decline a request for privileged attorney-client communications. Similarly, the United States may decline a request relating to a trade, business industrial, commercial or professional secret or information the disclosure of which would be contrary to public policy.

231.   However, communications between a client and an attorney or other admitted legal representative are, generally, only privileged to the extent that, the attorney or other legal representative acts in his or her capacity as an attorney or other legal representative. Where attorney – client privilege is more broadly defined it does not provide valid grounds on which to decline a request for exchange of information. To the extent, therefore, that an attor-ney acts as a nominee shareholder, a trustee, a settlor, a company director or under a power of attorney to represent a company in its business affairs, exchange of information resulting from and relating to any such activity cannot be declined because of the attorney-client privilege rule.

232.   Article 4 of the USA-Cayman Islands EOI agreement defines items subject to legal privilege as:

(a) *communications between an attorney-at-law and his client or any person representing his client made in connection with the giving of legal advice to the client;*

(a) *communications between an attorney-at-law and his client or any person representing his client or between such attorney-at-law or his client or any such representative and any other person made in connection with or in contemplation of legal proceedings and for the purposes of such proceedings; and*

(a) *items enclosed with or referred to in such communications and made –*

> (i)   *in connection with the giving of legal advice; or*
>
> (ii) *in connection with or in contemplation of legal proceedings and for the purposes of such proceedings,*
>
> *when they are in the possession of a person who is entitled to possession of them;*

but items held with the intention of furthering a criminal purpose are not subject to legal privilege.

233.   The United States' TIEA with the British Virgin Islands contains a similar provision. This definition appears to include information enclosed within a communication between an attorney and client and also within a communication between a client and another person who is not an attorney-at-law, which would be beyond the exemption for attorney client privilege under the international standard.

234.   The United States takes the view that this language merely extends the rule to include certain expert third parties, such as accountants, who are engaged by the attorney to assist in connection with (or in contemplation of) legal proceedings, consistent with U.S. law on attorney-client and is narrowly drawn by case law and based on a long-standing precedent (see Kovel v. United States, 296 F.2d 918 (2d Cir. 1961)). In practice, this aspect of the United States' agreements have not been an impediment to effective exchange of information.

Determination and factors underlying recommendations

Phase 1 Determination
The element is in place.

Phase 2 Rating
To be finalised as soon as a representative subset of Phase 2 reviews is completed

C.5. Timeliness of responses to requests for information

The jurisdiction should provide information under its network of agreements in a timely manner.

Responses within 90 days (ToR C.5.1.)

235.   The general proceduresfollowed by the EOI unit when a request is received from the foreign competent authority are as follows:

- Request assigned to EOI analyst
- Request reviewed and validated

- If request can be processed, and the information can be obtained from IRS databases

- Response prepared by EOI analyst and signed by U.S. Competent Authority or delegate and sent to foreign treaty partner.

236.   Where the information is in the hands of a governmental authority other than the IRS, the procedure and timelines followed are generally as above. In many cases, the information can be obtained through the use of a commercial database available to the IRS that provides direct access to information held by both government agencies and private sector information sources in the United States. Where the information requested includes state tax return information, the information is generally obtained and provided by the states via IRS's Federal/State Tax Exchange Program. The IRS has an exchange relationship with each of the 50 states. If information is requested that is in the possession of other Federal agencies, the information is sought through IRS's Federal/Federal Program. In these cases a period of approximately 45 days is required to obtain the information from the state or federal agency, as the case may be.

237.   Where the information is in the possession or control of a third party record-keeper, and it can be processed solely by EOI program, then an Information Document Request (IDR) is prepared and sent directly to the record keeper. The record keeper is normally asked to provide the requested information within 30 days. However extensions are occasionally granted when the information requested is complex and voluminous to avoid undue burden on the record keeper. Where the request requires field office assistance, then the request is sent to the appropriate field office for assignment. This will be the case when direct (in person) contact with the record-keeper may be necessary or other circumstances call for coordination with the field offices (*i.e.* ongoing examinations or investigation). In such cases the file is assigned either to a revenue agent in civil cases or to a special agent in criminal cases.

238.   Once the case has been assigned to an agent, then the agent contacts the taxpayer, prepares an Information Document Request (IDR), and attempts to obtain information from the taxpayer. If the information is obtained, then the agent transmits information back to the EOI analyst, which takes up to 30 days. A response is then prepared by EOI analyst and signed by U.S. Competent Authority or delegate and sent to foreign competent authority. For cases that can be processed solely by the EOI program, a response can be provided in about 90 days. If the case requires field office assistance, however, the response may take longer than 90 days. This final step takes up to 20 days. Summons Procedure

239.   If taxpayer/record keeper fails to respond to IDR, a summons will be issued. The EOI unit prepares the summons for Counsel review and approval. Once approval for the summons has been obtained, either the EOI analyst

sends summons to taxpayer or third-party and information is provided or, if the request requires field office assistance the summons is sent to field office for issuance to the taxpayer or third-party and information is provided. In rare cases where compliance with a summons is refused or challenged, additional time and resources will be required to enforce the summons. Once the information is in the hands of the agent it is sent to the EOI analyst. A response is then prepared by the EOI analyst and signed by the U.S. Competent Authority (or delegate) and sent to the foreign competent authority.

240.   Where the information is in the possession or control of a bank an IDR generally is not used. Instead, a summons is prepared and issued to the bank. Like all summonses on third parties, once a bank summons is issued the IRS provides banks with a standard period of time (generally 23 days) to respond. In the absence of a legal challenge, after the IRS issues a summons for banking information the recipient of the summons must produce the records requested within the time specified, which is generally less than 30 days after issuance. The information must then be processed back to the EOI analyst and a response prepared and signed by the U.S. Competent Authority (or delegate). A number of steps are involved and the approval of the summons itself can be a time-consuming process. Unavoidable delays are generally limited to cases where an IRS summons is challenged in court, which does not materialize in the vast majority of cases. A court inquiry is summary in nature, focused on confirming that the IRS summons satisfies the legal requirements for its issuance, which is generally determined based solely on the submission of sworn affidavits by the IRS. See U.S. v. Hiley, 2007 WL 2904056 (S.D. Cal. 2007).

241.   The majority of the United States' information exchange partners have expressed satisfaction with the quality and timeliness of the responses to their information requests. On average, the United States replies to approximately 1000 cases (each generally constituting multiple requests for information) per year, and automatically exchanges approximately 2.5 million items of information per year. For the combined review period, the United States reports that it fully responded within 90 days to more than 50% of specific requests (51%), within 180 days to more than 75% of specific requests (76%), and within 365 days to more than 90% of specific requests (91%). Input was provided by 24 partner jurisdictions regarding their exchange of information relationship with the United States. Generally, partner jurisdictions are satisfied with the timeliness of responses. Of the 24 peer inputs received, 19 peers identified no specific problems while 5 peers identified specific problems. In almost all cases the peers reported having a good exchange relationship with the United States. Some partners have indicated that response times are slow, in particular reference has been made to the lengthy nature of the summons process in the United States and delays in obtaining bank information. Some peers report that requests have gone unanswered and that no explanation has been provided by

the IRS. Others specifically cited the apparent difficulties of obtaining information concerning Delaware entities. As noted, the United States processes a large number of requests for information every year, and in some cases these requests involve very complex cases, may be incomplete, or involve supplemental requests, and delays may result in such circumstances. Peer jurisdictions have generally indicated that their relationship with the IRS is helpful and constructive, though it appears that improvements can be made to ensure exchange of information partners are informed in a timely manner of any difficulties in processing their requests. The US has advised that in response to the peer input obtained through the peer review process, it has amended its internal procedures to ensure that a notification with explanation is provided to its EOI partners if the request cannot be responded to within 90 days of receipt.

242.   The US provided information concerning 33 jurisdictions with which it has exchanged information more than three times over the past 3 years. The United States indicates that information was provided to all requesting jurisdictions most of the time. For one-third of the jurisdictions the United States provided information all of the time. The US further reports that, overall, information could not be provided in 7 percent of cases although, in their estimation, a substantial majority of these cases referred to circumstances where the information did not exist because the company in question did not exist or a purported transaction did not take place. In these cases the United States reported to the requesting jurisdiction that the entity did not exist or the purported transaction did not take place. Requests for information on LLCs only represents a fraction of the 7 percent figure cited above.

243.   The United States notes that delays generally are an inherent result of the caseloads borne by those working in exchange of information and that priorities must be established. Regarding delays in individual cases, the United States notes that this is difficult in the absence of the provision of identifying case numbers by the peers (which were not provided except in one case), particularly given the volume of requests processed each year by the IRS. Nevertheless, it appears that delays reported by the peers are consistent with the procedures cited above. There are a number of steps involved in each case, and the cumulative effect of the multiple deadlines means that a lengthy turnaround time is likely in many cases.

Organisational process and resources (ToR C.5.2.)

244.   The Deputy Commissioner (International), Large and Mid-Size Business division,[11] is delegated the authority to act as the U.S. Competent Authority under tax treaties and tax information exchange agreements pursuant

---

11.   As of 1 October 2010, the Large and Mid-Size Business operating division was realigned and renamed Large Business and International (LB&I). The new LB&I

to Delegation Order 4-12 (Revision 2). The Delegation Order further delegates authority to other officials with the Office of the Deputy Commissioner (International), LMSB to act as the U.S. competent authority for the Exchange of Information program. The official version of this Delegation Order is published in the Internal Revenue Manual and, therefore, is available to the general public.

245. The office of the U.S. Competent Authority consists of 24 employees who are actively involved with the Exchange of Information (EOI) Program on a daily basis. In addition to the employees utilized for EOI who directly report to the U.S. Competent Authority, the U.S. Competent Authority receives assistance in working EOI requests from revenue agents throughout the entire IRS, including the Small Business/Self-Employed and Large and Mid-Size Business operating divisions and, in the case of requests with criminal aspects, special agents from the Criminal Investigation Division.

246. In general, before being chosen for the EOI program, personnel have extensive experience in the IRS as revenue agents or similar career work in the IRS relating to tax compliance. Once employed in EOI, all employees receive classroom training, continuing professional education, and on-the-job training.

247. The identity of the United States Competent Authority is made known to all appropriate foreign tax officials either by the Office of the Deputy Commissioner (International), LMSB, the IRS's Tax Attachés, or the IRS Revenue Service Representative. The role of the U.S. Competent Authority, as well as procedures for handling foreign-initiated exchange-of-information requests, is generally described in various public web pages relating to international aspects of taxation is publicly available. The U.S. Competent Authority and his designated representatives maintain regular contact with their foreign competent authority counterparts throughout the world.

248. Resources available to the U.S. Competent Authority to service existing (or projected future) EOI requests include the following:

Financial

- Real estate – IRS provides the managers and employees who work EOI cases with modern office space and furniture in their post of duty.

---

organization will enhance the current International program, adding about 875 employees to the existing staff of nearly 600. Most of the additional examiners, economists and technical staff are current employees who specialize on international issues within other parts of LMSB.

- Computers – The managers and employees have IRS laptops or desktops and receive support from the IRS's Modernization and Information Technology Services department (MITS) within the U.S. as well as overseas.

- Costs for issuing summonses, obtaining records, and database subscriptions etc. – IRS has funding available to cover these charges and simple processes for obtaining it.

- Salaries and Benefits – IRS funding for salaries and benefits is sufficient to cover costs including annual cost of living increases and performance awards.

- Travel Funds – IRS funds the travel expenses of technical advisors, EOI analysts/managers and tax attachés to work EOI in offices in Washington, DC and overseas.

Technical

- The IRS's *Integrated Data Retrieval System (IDRS)* is an internal IRS database available to personnel who work EOI cases for the IRS. This system shows the federal income tax accounts of all taxpayers and the status of their tax filing and payment obligations in the U.S. Access to any given account is on a need-to-know basis only. A wide variety of other investigative tools are also available, including a database that provides a full suite of investigative tools to government entities, including the IRS, enabling users to quickly access a wide range of information held by various government agencies.

- Internal Revenue Manual 4.60.1 (*Exchange of Information*) provides guidance to employees who work EOI cases.

Personnel

- The IRS has divided the specific EOI requests by country and/or issue among seven offices. Headquarters for the U.S. Competent Authority is in Washington, DC, and the IRS has representatives for the U.S. Competent Authority throughout the U.S. and the world. A Revenue Service Representative is in Plantation, Florida, and there are Tax Attachés in London, U.K.; Paris, France; Frankfurt, Germany; and Beijing, China. Each office has additional employees who work for the U.S. Competent Authority. In addition, the headquarters office employs an EOI tax specialist in El Segundo, California.

- Most of the EOI analysts are former Revenue Agents with University-level degrees, who are required to have a minimum of 24 credit hours of college-level accounting classes.

- Additionally, at present, the U.S. Competent Authority is recruiting persons to fill open positions in the EOI program.

- The U.S. Competent Authority also enjoys access to revenue agents, revenue officers, and criminal investigation agents throughout the primary operating divisions in the Internal Revenue Service. In general, personnel throughout the IRS are obliged to assist the U.S. Competent Authority on exchange-of-information matters.

249.   Specialized exchange-of-information training concerning the IRS's information-gathering obligations under EOI mechanisms, procedures for internal processing of requests, and obligations for maintaining confidentiality of treaty communications is conducted for all new EOI managers, tax law specialists and analysts. The training consists of on-line, classroom, and on-the-job training. Continuing professional education on EOI is also provided to experienced analysts on a consistent basis. Other sources of administrative guidance and internal procedures include IRM 4.60.1 (Exchange of Information) and the Exchange of Information Handbook that is available to all EOI analysts.

250.   All new analysts to HQ, technical advisors in the Joint International Tax Shelter Information Centre (JITSIC), and new tax attachés (approximately 20 over the last three years) attend an EOI overview course that is delivered in Washington, DC by experienced managers, analysts, and IRS Chief Counsel attorneys. Analysts hired directly at the posts receive overview training at their posts. All then receive on-the-job training by the experienced personnel around them (*e.g.* HQ by other HQ personnel, post employees by other post personnel.) The EOI Program also delivers Continuing Professional Education (CPE) regarding information exchange and specific issues therein at various IRS CPEs.

251.   For many years the IRS used a locally-developed database to control and monitor (track) requests received from and sent to Treaty/TIEA partners. This database was accessible by all IRS offices responsible for EOI. In October of 2009, a new tracking system was brought on-line that replaced the "old database." Basically, both databases track all relevant information for the United States EOI program.

252.   The IRS measures its performance based on the factual data the IRS systems collect and analyze. Reports are produced that allow managers to assess performance of the EOI program, including measures based on the numbers and types of cases processed, time to process a case, current case status, country involved, category of information requested, and whether a summons is necessary to obtain information.

Absence of restrictive conditions on exchange of information (ToR C.5.3.)

253.   Exchange of information with the United States is not hindered by any restrictive conditions.

Determination and factors underlying recommendations

Determination
The assessment team is not in a position to evaluate whether this element is in place, as it involves issues of practice that are dealt with in the Phase 2 review.

Rating
To be finalised as soon as a representative subset of Phase 2 reviews is completed

Factors underlying recommendations	Recommendations
A number of the United States partners have pointed to delays in obtaining information and the procedures for responding to requests, which require a number of steps, appear to inhibit response times.	The United States should examine how its competent authority could speed up its internal processes for obtaining and providing information to ensure more timely responses and provide a status update within 90 days in all cases.

Summary of Determinations
and Factors Underlying Recommendations[12]

Determination	Factors underlying recommendations	Recommendations
Jurisdictions should ensure that ownership and identity information for all relevant entities and arrangements is available to their competent authorities. *(ToR A.1)*		
Phase 1 Determination: The element is in place, but certain aspects of the legal implementation of the element need improvement.	Ownership and identity information for single member LLCs is not always available	The United States should take all necessary steps to ensure that information concerning the owners of all LLCs is available.
Phase 2 Rating: To be completed once a representative subset of Phase 2 reviews have been completed.		
Jurisdictions should ensure that reliable accounting records are kept for all relevant entities and arrangements. *(ToR A.2)*		
Phase 1 Determination: The element is in place, but certain aspects of the legal implementation of the element need improvement.	Accounting information for all single member LLCs is not always available.	The United States should ensure that accounting records (including underlying documentation) are available for all LLCs.
Phase 2 Rating: To be completed once a representative subset of Phase 2 reviews have been completed.		

12. The ratings will be finalised as soon as a representative subset of Phase 2 reviews is completed.

Determination	Factors underlying recommendations	Recommendations
Banking information should be available for all account-holders. (ToR A.3)		
Phase 1 Determination: The element is in place.		
Phase 2 Rating: To be completed once a representative subset of Phase 2 reviews have been completed.		
Competent authorities should have the power to obtain and provide information that is the subject of a request under an exchange of information arrangement from any person within their territorial jurisdiction who is in possession or control of such information (irrespective of any legal obligation on such person to maintain the secrecy of the information). *(ToR B.1)*		
Phase 1 Determination: The element is in place.		
Phase 2 Rating: To be completed once a representative subset of Phase 2 reviews have been completed.		
The rights and safeguards (*e.g.* notification, appeal rights) that apply to persons in the requested jurisdiction should be compatible with effective exchange of information. *(ToR B.2)*		
Phase 1 Determination: The element is in place.		
Phase 2 Rating: To be completed once a representative subset of Phase 2 reviews have been completed.		

Determination	Factors underlying recommendations	Recommendations
Exchange of information mechanisms should allow for effective exchange of information. *(ToR C.1)*		
Phase 1 Determination: The element is in place.		
Phase 2 Rating: To be completed once a representative subset of Phase 2 reviews have been completed.		
The jurisdictions' network of information exchange mechanisms should cover all relevant partners. *(ToR C.2)*		
Phase 1 Determination: The element is in place.		The United States should continue to develop its EOI network with all relevant partners.
Phase 2 Rating: To be completed once a representative subset of Phase 2 reviews have been completed.		
The jurisdictions' mechanisms for exchange of information should have adequate provisions to ensure the confidentiality of information received. *(ToR C.3)*		
Phase 1 Determination: The element is in place.		
Phase 2 Rating: To be completed once a representative subset of Phase 2 reviews have been completed.		

Determination	Factors underlying recommendations	Recommendations
The exchange of information mechanisms should respect the rights and safeguards of taxpayers and third parties. *(ToR C.4)*		
Phase 1 Determination: The element is in place.		
Phase 2 Rating: To be completed once a representative subset of Phase 2 reviews have been completed.		
The jurisdiction should provide information under its network of agreements in a timely manner. *(ToR C.5)*		
Phase 1 Determination: The assessment team is not in a position to evaluate whether this element is in place, as it involves issues of practice that are dealt with in the Phase 2 review.		
Phase 2 Rating: To be completed once a representative subset of Phase 2 reviews have been completed.	A number of the United States partners have pointed to delays in obtaining information and the procedures for responding to requests, which require a number of steps, appear to inhibit response times.	The United States should examine how its competent authority could speed up its internal processes for obtaining and providing information to ensure more timely responses and provide a status update within 90 days in all cases.

Annex 1: Jurisdiction's Response to the Review Report*

This annex is left blank because the United States of America has chosen not to provide any material to include in it.

---

* This Annex presents the Jurisdiction's response to the review report and shall not be deemed to represent the Global Forum's views.

Annex 2: List of all Exchange-of-Information Mechanisms in Force

	Jurisdiction	Type of EoI Arrangement	Date Signed	Date Entered Into Force
1	Australia	DTC (+Protocol)	06-Aug-82	01-Dec-83
2	Austria	DTC	31-May-96	01-Jan-99
3	Bahamas	TIEA	25-Jan-02	01-Jan-06
4	Bangladesh	DTC	26-Sep-04	07-Aug-06
5	Barbados	DTC (+Protocols)	31-Dec-84	28-Feb-86
	Barbados	TIEA	03-Nov-84	03-Nov-84
6	Belgium	DTC (+Protocol)	27-Nov-06	28-Dec-07
7	Bermuda	DTC	11-Jul-86	02-Dec-88
	Bermuda	TIEA	02-Dec-88	02-Dec-88
8	Brazil	TIEA	20-Mar-06	Not in force
9	British Virgin Islands	TIEA	03-Apr-02	01-Jan-04
10	Bulgaria	DTC (+Protocols)	23-Feb-07	15-Dec-08
11	Canada	DTC (+Protocols)	26-Sep-80	16-Aug-84
12	Cayman Islands	TIEA	27-Nov-01	10-Mar-06
13	Chile	DTC	04-Feb-10	Not in force
14	China	DTC (+Protocols)	30-Apr-84	22-Oct-86
15	Colombia	TIEA	30-Mar-01	Not in force
16	Costa Rica	TIEA	15-Mar-89	12-Feb-91
17	Cyprus [13, 14]	DTC	19-Mar-84	31-Dec-85

13. Note by Turkey: The information in this document with reference to "Cyprus" relates to the southern part of the Island. There is no single authority representing both Turkish and Greek Cypriot people on the Island. Turkey recognises the Turkish Republic of Northern Cyprus (TRN C). Until a lasting and equitable solution is found within the context of the United Nations, Turkey shall preserve its position concerning the "Cyprus issue".

14. Note by all the European Union Member States of the OECD and the European Commission: The Republic of Cyprus is recognised by all members of the United Nations with the exception of Turkey. The information in this document relates to the area under the effective control of the Government of the Republic of Cyprus.

	Jurisdiction	Type of EoI Arrangement	Date Signed	Date Entered Into Force
18	Czech Republic	DTC	16-Sep-93	23-Dec-93
19	Denmark	DTC (+Protocols)	19-Aug-99	29-Jan-01
20	Dominica	TIEA	01-Oct-87	09-May-88
21	Dominican Republic	TIEA	07-Aug-89	12-Oct-89
22	Egypt	DTC	24-Aug-80	31-Dec-81
23	Estonia	DTC	15-Jan-98	01-Jan-00
24	Finland	DTC (+Protocol)	21-Sep-89	01-Jan-91
25	France	DTC (+Protocols)	31-Aug-94	30-Dec-95
26	Germany	DTC (+Protocols)	29-Aug-89	01-Jan-91
27	Gibraltar	TIEA	01-Mar-09	22-Dec-09
28	Greece	DTC	20-Feb-50	01-Jan-53
29	Grenada	TIEA	18-Dec-86	13-Jul-87
30	Guernsey	TIEA	19-Sep-02	30-Mar-06
31	Guyana	TIEA	22-Jul-92	27-Aug-92
32	Honduras	TIEA	27-Sep-90	11-Oct-91
33	Hungary	DTC	12-Feb-79	18-Sep-79
	Hungary	DTC	04-Feb-10	Not in force
34	Iceland	DTC (+Protocol)	23-Oct-07	15-Dec-08
35	India	DTC	12-Sep-89	01-Jan-91
36	Indonesia	DTC	11-Jul-88	01-Jan-90
37	Ireland	DTC	28-Jul-97	01-Jan-98
38	Isle of Man	TIEA	03-Oct-02	01-Jan-06
39	Israel	DTC (+Protocols)	20-Nov-75	01-Jan-95
40	Italy	DTC (+Protocol)	25-Aug-99	16-Dec-09
41	Jamaica	DTC	21-May-80	29-Dec-81
	Jamaica	TIEA	18-Dec-03	18-Dec-03
42	Japan	DTC (+Protocol)	06-Nov-03	30-Mar-04
43	Jersey	TIEA	04-Nov-02	26-Jun-06
44	Kazakhstan	DTC (+Protocol)	24-Oct-93	01-Jan-96
45	Latvia	DTC	15-Jan-98	01-Jan-00
46	Liechtenstein	TIEA	08-Dec-08	04-Dec-09
47	Lithuania	DTC	15-Jan-98	01-Jan-00

	Jurisdiction	Type of EoI Arrangement	Date Signed	Date Entered Into Force
48	Luxembourg	DTC	03-Apr-96	01-Jan-01
	Luxembourg	Protocol	20-May-09	Not in force
49	Malta	DTC	08-Aug-08	
50	Marshall Islands	TIEA	14-Mar-91	14-Mar-91
51	Mexico	DTC (+Protocol)	18-Sep-92	01-Jan-94
	Mexico	TIEA	09-Nov-89	18-Jan-90
52	Monaco	TIEA	08-Sep-09	11-Mar-10
53	Morocco	DTC	01-Aug-77	30-Dec-81
54	Netherlands	DTC (+Protocol)	18-Dec-92	01-Jan-94
55	Netherlands Antilles	TIEA	17-Apr-02	22-Mar-07
56	New Zealand	DTC	23-Jul-82	02-Nov-83
	New Zealand	Protocol	01-Dec-08	Not in force
57	Norway	DTC	03-Dec-71	29-Nov-72
58	Pakistan	DTC	01-Jul-57	21-May-59
59	Peru	TIEA	15-Feb-90	31-Mar-93
60	Philippines	DTC	01-Oct-76	16-Oct-82
61	Poland	DTC	08-Oct-74	22-Jul-76
62	Portugal	DTC	06-Sep-94	01-Jan-96
63	Romania	DTC	04-Dec-73	26-Feb-76
64	Russia	DTC	17-Jun-92	01-Jan-94
65	Slovak Republic	DTC	08-Oct-93	30-Dec-93
66	Slovenia	DTC	21-Jun-99	22-Jun-01
67	South Africa	DTC	17-Feb-97	28-Dec-97
68	South Korea	DTC	04-Jun-76	20-Sep-79
69	Spain	DTC	22-Feb-90	21-Nov-90
70	Sri Lanka	DTC (+Protocol)	14-Mar-85	12-Jul-04
71	Sweden	DTC (+Protocol)	01-Sep-94	26-Oct-95
72	Switzerland	DTC	02-Oct-96	01-Jan-98
	Switzerland	Protocol	23-Sep-09	Not in force
73	Thailand	DTC	26-Nov-96	15-Dec-97
74	Trinidad & Tobago	DTC	09-Jan-70	30-Dec-70
	Trinidad & Tobago	TIEA	11-Jan-89	09-Feb-90

	Jurisdiction	Type of EoI Arrangement	Date Signed	Date Entered Into Force
75	Tunisia	DTC	17-Jun-85	26-Dec-90
76	Turkey	DTC	28-Mar-96	19-Dec-97
77	Ukraine	DTC	04-Mar-94	05-Jun-00
78	United Kingdom	DTC (+Protocol)	24-Jul-01	31-Mar-03
79	Venezuela	DTC	25-Jan-99	30-Dec-99

Annex 3: List of all Laws, Regulations and Other Relevant Material

Tax laws

Internal Revenue Code and Regulations

Relevant tax forms and schedules

Relevant case law

Company Laws

Model Business Corporation Act (MBCA)

Delaware General Company Law

California Corporations Code

New York Business Corporations Law 2001

Pennsylvania Corporations and Unincorporated Associations Law

Florida Business Corporations Act

Texas Business Organizations Code

Securities Exchange Act of 1934

Securities Act of 1933

Bank Secrecy Act (BSA)

Partnerships

Uniform Limited Partnership Act (2001)

Delaware Limited Partnership Act

Texas Business Organizations Code, ch. 153, title 4

Pennsylvania Statutes Title 15

Revised Uniform Limited Liability Company Act (2006)

Delaware Limited Liability Company Act

California Limited Liability Company Act

Florida Limited Liability Company Act

New York Texas Limited Liability Company Act

Texas Limited Liability Company Act

Trusts

Restatement Third, Trusts

Uniform Trust Code

Restatement (Second) of Conflict of Laws

Relevant case law

Annex 4: People Interviewed during On-Site Visit

Representatives from the U.S. Treasury Department

Representatives from the Internal Revenue Service including:

- The Deputy Commissioner (International), Large and Mid-Size Business division (the U.S. competent authority)
- Director Treaty Administration & Int'l Coordination
- Revenue Service Representative Plantation, FL
- IRS Chief Counsel attorneys

Representatives of FinCEN

ORGANISATION FOR ECONOMIC CO-OPERATION AND DEVELOPMENT

The OECD is a unique forum where governments work together to address the economic, social and environmental challenges of globalisation. The OECD is also at the forefront of efforts to understand and to help governments respond to new developments and concerns, such as corporate governance, the information economy and the challenges of an ageing population. The Organisation provides a setting where governments can compare policy experiences, seek answers to common problems, identify good practice and work to co-ordinate domestic and international policies.

The OECD member countries are: Australia, Austria, Belgium, Canada, Chile, the Czech Republic, Denmark, Estonia, Finland, France, Germany, Greece, Hungary, Iceland, Ireland, Israel, Italy, Japan, Korea, Luxembourg, Mexico, the Netherlands, New Zealand, Norway, Poland, Portugal, the Slovak Republic, Slovenia, Spain, Sweden, Switzerland, Turkey, the United Kingdom and the United States. The European Commission takes part in the work of the OECD.

OECD Publishing disseminates widely the results of the Organisation's statistics gathering and research on economic, social and environmental issues, as well as the conventions, guidelines and standards agreed by its members.

OECD PUBLISHING, 2, rue André-Pascal, 75775 PARIS CEDEX 16
(23 2011 32 1 P) ISBN 978-92-64-11505-7 – No. 58187 2011-01